THE SPO

(SKIATHOS, SKOPELOS, ALO

AN ISLAND-HOPPING ADVENTURE GUIDE

RENE HOOVER

DISCLAIMER

The information in this travel guide is for general informational purposes only. While we strive for accuracy, travel conditions, regulations, and safety guidelines may change without notice. Readers are encouraged to verify details with official sources before making travel plans. The authors and publishers are not responsible for any errors, omissions, injuries, losses, or inconveniences resulting from the use of this guide. Travel responsibly and at your own risk.

ACKNOWLEDGEMENTS AND GRATITUDE

This book would not have been possible without the support of many wonderful people. I deeply thank my family—especially my partner for unwavering encouragement, and my parents and children, whose love inspires me every day.

I am equally grateful to my mentors, friends, and the entire publishing team for their invaluable feedback and steadfast support. Your guidance, whether through kind words, practical advice, or creative collaboration, has shaped every page of this work.

Lastly, thank you to you, the reader, for joining me on this journey. Your curiosity and passion for discovery are what make all of this worthwhile.

Rene Hoover

ABOUT THE AUTHOR

Rene Hoover is an explorer at heart, a storyteller whose passion for discovering the world shines through every page of his guide books. Born with a curiosity and a desire to experience life beyond borders, Rene has journeyed far and wide—from the bustling streets of international metropolises to the hidden corners of quaint villages.

His travel guides are not just collections of tips and recommendations; they're windows into new cultures, adventures, and the countless stories that make each place unique.

When he's not on the road, Rene can be found planning his next expedition, poring over maps and local histories, or connecting with fellow travelers and locals to unearth the hidden gems of each region. With a deep respect for sustainable and responsible travel, he strives to inspire others to explore the world thoughtfully and with an open heart.

Through his engaging travel guides and captivating narratives, Rene Hoover continues to transform the way we experience our world—one unforgettable journey at a time.

TABLE OF CONTENTS

INTRODUCTION

The Sporades islands are a group of four main islands located along the eastern coast of Greece. They include Skiathos, Skopelos, Alonissos, and Skyros. Each island has its own unique character, ranging from lively beaches with vibrant bars to quiet, peaceful spots surrounded by pine trees.

The sweet spot for island-hopping is between mid-April and late October, when the weather is warm, the sea is crystal-clear, and the ferry network is in full swing. Outside these months, many tavernas and hotels close up shop, so if you're craving "island time," aim for spring blossoms or the late-summer lull.

Skiathos is often your gateway: direct flights from Athens, Thessaloniki, or even London drops you into Skiathos Town, where scooters zip past pastel waterfront cafés.

Beach lovers, you're in heaven—don't miss *Koukounaries Beach* (ideal for early-morning swims), *Stafilos* (family-friendly sandy bay), and the otherworldly *Lalaria*, with its white-pebble shores and cliff-framed entrance that's only boat-accessible.

When the sun dips below the horizon, Skiathos Town lights up with welcoming ouzo bars, live music spots, and little tavernas serving freshly grilled octopus.

Hop next to Skopelos, the lush "pine-forest island" you might recognize from **Mamma Mia!** The inner bays like *Kastani* and *Panormos* feature shallow, safe waters perfect for snorkelling or paddleboarding, while the island's spine is crisscrossed by scenic hiking trails through fragrant pines.

In Skopelos Town, pastel neoclassical mansions line narrow lanes draped in bougainvillea—ideal for an afternoon gelato crawl. Look out for local bakeries dishing up *bougatsa* (cream-filled phyllo) and charming seaside spots where a glass of rosé feels like liquid sunshine.

For a change of pace, Alonissos beckons with Europe's largest marine protected area. Here, boat tours glide past monk-seal haunts and dolphins that might race your kee. Snorkellers and divers will find coral beds teeming with tiny fish, while on land the old town's windy, cobbled alleys offer panoramic sea views and authentic tavernas where you can taste island-foraged capers and olives.

Eco-friendly lodgings have popped up recently, so you can rest easy knowing your stay supports conservation.

Finally, Skyros—the archipelago's southern outlier—is a blend of rugged hills and sandy shores. Skyros Town's whitewashed houses and red-tiled roofs spill down to a sheltered harbor, luring you into artisan workshops where you can watch traditional woodcarving or buy the island's famed Skyrian ponies in miniature form.

The island's north is surprisingly mountainous, perfect for sunrise hikes, while the south features family-friendly beaches like *Magazia* and *Agios Petros*.

Logistics & Tips: A classic loop is 4 nights on Skiathos, 3 on Skopelos, 2 in Alonissos, and 2 in Skyros—then back to Volos or Volos airport via ferry. Ferries run daily in high season, with high-speed catamarans shaving travel times.

Consider booking 2–3 weeks out for best fares, and keep a flexible mindset—weather or sea conditions can shuffle schedules. Pack reef-friendly sunscreen, sturdy sandals for pebbly beaches, and a reusable water bottle: these islands reward curious, eco-minded travelers. Safe travels and happy hopping!

HOW TO USE THIS BOOK

Welcome to your travel companion for exploring the Greek Sporades. This guide is designed to be your hands-on tool for discovering hidden gems, practical tips, and vibrant local stories. Here's how to get the most out of your journey:

Navigating the Multimedia Codes

Scattered throughout the book are QR Codes that unlock a wealth of digital content:

Interactive Maps: Easily locate attractions and plan routes with detailed maps that show nearby points of interest.

Pictures and Videos: Get a visual preview of each destination—from panoramic views and local landmarks to cultural events—helping you to decide where to focus your time.

Additional Insider Tips: Access extended travel tips, local restaurant recommendations, and seasonal advice that will enhance your experience.

To use the QR Codes, simply open your smartphone's camera or a QR scanner app and point it at the code. Follow the link to explore interactive content that brings each attraction to life.

Custom Experiences: Some sections also suggest local events and seasonal activities that are not widely advertised. These tips help you see the Sporades from a local's point of view, making your trip truly unique.

Who This Guide Is For?

This travel guide is crafted for anyone with a spirit of adventure:

Independent Explorers: If you enjoy planning your own route and discovering hidden corners, this guide will be your reliable resource.

Cultural Enthusiasts: For those interested in history, local legends, and the authentic charm of Greek island life, every page offers insights into the traditions and everyday stories of the Sporades.

Families and Solo Travelers: Whether you're planning a family vacation or a solo retreat, the easy-to-follow maps, insider tips, and multimedia links ensure you have a well-rounded and enjoyable experience.

Curious Minds: Even if you're comparing travel spots or planning a future trip to places like the Sporades, our guide offers a bridge between cultures—showing how different destinations can inspire one another.

We hope this guide serves as both a practical tool and an invitation to explore more deeply than any brochure ever could. Enjoy your journey, and let every page lead you to a new adventure!

WHY THE SPORADES? (OVERVIEW OF THE ARCHIPELAGO IN THE AEGEAN SEA)

The Sporades—Greece's island-hopping secret that's equal parts lush, lively, and laced with legend. Tucked into the Aegean's sparkling embrace, this scattered archipelago (the name literally means "those scattered ones") feels like the Mediterranean's best-kept secret.

But let's be real: once you've dipped your toes into its pine-fringed coves or sailed past uninhabited islets where wild goats outnumber people, you'll wonder why it took you so long to discover it.

Imagine four main islands—Skiathos, Skopelos, Alonissos, and Skyros—each with its own unique charm, along with a few small, peaceful islands that feel like hidden treasures.

They're not your typical Cycladic postcard; forget whitewashed villages (well, mostly). Instead, you get emerald forests tumbling down to turquoise bays, medieval castles perched on cliffs, and beaches so quiet you'll hear the cicadas over the waves.

And because they're spread across the northern Aegean, just a stone's throw from mainland Greece, they're surprisingly accessible for a taste of off-the-beaten-path adventure.

Let's start with the vibe. The Sporades are the Aegean's green queens. Think dense pine forests that scent the air like a Christmas tree farm in July, olive groves that have been around since ancient times, and valleys bursting with almond blossoms.

Skiathos, the life of the party, balances buzzy beach bars with hidden trails through its UNESCO-protected wetlands.

Skopelos, the drama queen, served as the backdrop for **Mamma Mia!** and still struts its stuff with cobblestone streets and Byzantine monasteries clinging to hillsides.

Alonissos, the eco-warrior, is a sanctuary for rare seabirds and dolphins, thanks to the *Northern Sporades National Marine Park*—the largest in Europe.

And then there's Skyros, the rebel, where you'll find wild horses roaming the hills and a castle that's been standing since the Venetians ruled the waves.

Here's the thing: the Sporades aren't just about good looks. They give you a true taste of authentic Greek island living. You're not going to run into packed tourist spots everywhere (okay, maybe on Skiathos during August, but that's an exception we can live with).

Instead, you'll sip *ouzo* with fishermen in Skopelos' harbor, learn to make *sporadia* (traditional cheese pies) from a grandmother in Alonissos, or stumble upon a centuries-old olive press turned art gallery.

The islands wear their history lightly—like that cool vintage jacket you found at a flea market—but it's there if you look.

Skyros' ancient shipbuilding traditions? Still alive. The myths of pirates and poets? Alive in the locals' stories.

And let's talk logistics, because island-hopping here is a breeze. Ferries zip between the main islands in under an hour, so you can easily base yourself in one spot or island-hop daily.

Want a lazy beach day? *Plaka Beach* on Alonissos has waters so clear you'll think someone Photoshopped them.

Craving a hike? Skiathos' hidden coves reward the adventurous with solitude and snorkeling spots.

 Feeling fancy? Skyros' luxury villas blend seamlessly into the rugged landscape.

The cherry on top? The Sporades are having a moment. New eco-conscious resorts are popping up, offering solar-powered stays and farm-to-table feasts. Local artisans are reviving ancient crafts, from Skyros' intricate woodcarvings to Skopelos' pottery workshops. Even the food scene is leveling up—think sea urchin pasta in Alonissos and Skiathos' famous sundried tomato keftedes (meatballs).

So why the Sporades? Because they're Greece unplugged. A place where you can island-hop without the crowds, dive into crystal-clear waters, and still catch that sunset from a mountaintop taverna—all while feeling like you've stepped into a slower, saltier, more authentic version of the Aegean dream.

Pack your swimsuit, a good pair of hiking shoes, and a sense of curiosity. Trust us, your Instagram feed (and your soul) will thank you.

PLANNING YOUR TRIP

When to Visit (Seasonal Weather, Crowds & Festival Calendar)

Timing is everything when it comes to the Sporades—get it right, and you'll glide between islands like a local; get it wrong, and you might end up elbow-to-elbow with half of Europe on Skiathos' *Banana Beach*. Let's break down the when, why, and how to plan your island-hopping adventure like a seasoned insider.

The Sweet Spot: May–June & September–October

If you're after that golden blend of good weather, manageable crowds, and authentic vibes, aim for late spring or early autumn.

In May and June, the islands shake off their winter slumber—wildflowers carpet Skopelos' hillsides, the sea warms to a refreshing 22°C (72°F), and locals are still in "slow island mode".

By September, the summer chaos melts away, leaving behind glassy waters perfect for snorkeling and empty trails begging for hikes. Plus, you'll snag better deals on villas and boutique stays.

Just pack a light jacket for evenings; the meltemi winds can kick up a breeze, especially on Alonissos.

Peak Season: July–August (Proceed with Caution)

July and August are the Sporades' blockbuster months—think 30°C (86°F) sunshine, beach bars blasting Greek pop, and ferries packed like sardines.

Skiathos transforms into a nightlife hotspot, with crowds spilling out of cocktail bars until dawn. If you're craving energy and don't mind jostling for a sunbed, this is your window.

But here's the local lowdown: book everything — ferries, hotels, even that coveted table at Skopelos' waterfront tavernas—weeks in advance.

And if you're island-hopping, prioritize mornings for ferry departures; afternoon routes often sell out.

Winter? Not So Much

The Sporades aren't exactly a winter wonderland. Most islands hibernate from November to April, with ferries running sporadically (pun intended) and many businesses shuttered.

Skyros, the outlier, stays mildly active thanks to its winter carnival and a handful of cozy guesthouses, but even there, you'll need a car to navigate rain-slicked roads.

Save this for die-hard off-season explorers.

Festivals & Hidden Gems

Timing your trip around local festivals? You're in luck. Skiathos throws a lively *Anthestiria* flower festival in May, while Skopelos honors its patron saint, **Agios Riginos**, with processions and feasts in late August.

Alonissos' eco-conscious crowd celebrates **World Oceans Day** in June with beach clean-ups and marine talks—a quieter but deeply meaningful way to connect with the islands.

Tip: Ask your host or a taverna owner about village *panigiria* (festivals). These pop-up parties, often tied to harvests or saints' days, are where you'll devour wood-fired *koulouri* (sesame bread) and dance to lyra music with the locals.

Weather vs. Water

The Sporades' microclimates keep things interesting. Skiathos and Skopelos, being more sheltered, tend to have calmer seas—ideal for kayaking or paddleboarding.

Alonissos and Skyros, exposed to the Aegean's open waters, can get breezy, but that's part of the charm (hello, windsurfing!).

Sea temperatures peak in August, but even in October, you'll find brave souls swimming in sheltered bays like *Panormos* on Skopelos.

Local Logistics

Ferries are the heartbeat of Sporades travel, but schedules shift with the seasons. In peak summer, you can island-hop daily—say, Skiathos to Skopelos in 45 minutes, or Alonissos to Skyros in a leisurely 2.5 hours.

Come September, routes thin out, so plan buffer days in case of delays.

If you're thinking of renting a vehicle, Skyros needs a car because of its rough terrain, but on Skiathos, it's better to go with a scooter—watch out for heavy traffic in July.

The Unwritten Rules

Here's what the guidebooks won't tell you: On Skopelos, the real sunset views are from the chapel of *Agios Ioannis*, not the crowded port.

In Alonissos, ask fishermen about "secret" coves— some will share GPS coordinates for a euro or two.

And if you're on Skyros in August, avoid the main port town on weekends when day-trippers flood the island.

Budgeting & Money (Daily Costs, ATMs & Currency Exchange)

Alright, let's talk euros and sense—because even in paradise, budgets matter. The Sporades might feel like a wallet-friendly escape compared to Santorini's glitz, but a little local know-how goes a long way. Here's how to stretch your euros without skimping on that sunset cocktail or hidden cove kayak trip.

Daily Costs: What's the Damage?

Let's get real: the Sporades aren't cheap, but they're far from the priciest Greek islands. A rough daily estimate hovers around 120–150€ per person if you're staying in mid-range hotels, eating taverna meals, and hopping ferries.

Here's a local tip: cut costs where it really matters. Skip the expensive bars at Banana Beach on Skiathos—where drinks can cost up to 10€—and head instead to small neighborhood spots where you can grab a frappé for just 2€ and a souvlaki wrap for 5€.

On Alonissos, lunch at a family-run *psistaria* (grill house) costs half what you'd pay at a waterfront spot—plus, you'll get a free shot of sour cherry tsipouro to seal the deal.

Ferries: The Hidden Budget Hack

Island-hopping costs add up, but the Sporades' compact size works in your favor.

Public ferries between Skiathos, Skopelos, and Alonissos cost 25–35€ round-trip,—a steal compared to the Cyclades. Book early in peak season (July–August) to snag seats, or risk last-minute scrambles.

Tip: Sail from Vourvourou on the mainland to Skiathos early in the morning for 30€ and avoid the Volos crowds.

For Skyros, budget extra: the longer ferry ride from Alonissos clocks in around 45€, but the island's wild horses and car-free villages are worth every euro.

Cash is King (and ATMs are Moody)

Cards work in bigger towns, but carry cash for small islands and tavernas. ATMs on Skiathos and Skopelos are reliable, but Alonissos has just two—and they've been known to empty by midday in August.

Exchange euros before arriving; airport kiosks gouge rates. If you're flying into Skiathos, hit the ATM at the port before ferries arrive to beat the crowds. And forget traveler's checks—locals will stare at them like you're offering drachmas.

Eat Like a Local, Spend Like a Local

The Sporades' food scene is a budget traveler's dream—if you play it smart.

Breakfast? Grab a 1.50€ *koulouri* (sesame bread ring) from a bakery and eat it on the beach.

Lunch? Follow the fishermen to Skopelos' harbor tavernas for 8€ grilled octopus fresh off the boat.

Dinner? Skyros' village squares dish out 10€ meatball platters with a side of live lyra music.

Avoid tourist traps with English menus—look for places where grandmas are rolling dough or frying *keftedes* (meatballs) in the back.

Hidden Costs (and How to Dodge Them)

Scooters vs. Cars: On Skiathos, a scooter rental is 15€/day —perfect for zipping to secret beaches.

On Skyros, you'll need a car (40€/day) to explore the rugged interior.

Beach Clubs: Those plush sunbeds on Skiathos' *Koukounaries Beach?* They're 12€ a pop. Pack a towel and claim a free patch of sand instead.

Festival FOMO: Attending a *panigiria* (village festival)? Entrance is free, but you'll shell out 20€+ for a night of feasting and dancing—worth it for the insider vibes.

Budget-Friendly Hacks

Stay Local: Skip Skiathos' luxury resorts and rent a room from a 25€/night family pension on Skopelos—breakfast (and gossip) included.

BYO Everything: Shops on Alonissos sell wine for 5€ a bottle —stock up for sunset picnics.

Off-Season Deals: Visit in May or September for 40% off villa prices and empty trails.

The Travelex Trick

Can't stomach carrying wads of cash? Load a *Travelex Money Card* with euros before you go—tap-and-go at tavernas, ferries, and even Skyros' artisan workshops. It's safer than cash and avoids dynamic currency conversion scams.

Final Word to the Wise

The Sporades won't break the bank if you embrace their rhythm. Bargain at markets (yes, even for that "antique" olive jar), tip waiters in cash (round up the bill), and always—always —carry a 2€ coin for emergency ice cream.

Because when a gelato costs less than a postcard, you might as well eat your way through the islands.

Bottom line? Spend smart, eat local, and let the Aegean breeze blow your budget worries away. These islands have a way of making even the thriftiest traveler feel like a millionaire—no yacht required.

Essential Packing List (Clothing, Gear for Hiking/Diving, Sun Protection)

Alright, let's dive into the packing puzzle for the Sporades—because showing up with just a swimsuit and a smile might leave you scrambling when you're hiking Skopelos' pine trails or dodging sea urchins in Alonissos' coves.

Here's the local lowdown on what to stuff in your bag (and what to leave behind).

Clothing: Light, Layered, and Ready for Anything

The Sporades' dress code is "island casual"—think breezy linens, quick-dry fabrics, and layers for those unpredictable Aegean mood swings.

Start with lightweight pants or flowy maxi dresses for taverna dinners, but toss in a windbreaker or waterproof jacket for evenings when the meltemi winds decide to show off.

Hiking? Swap flip-flops for sturdy sandals or lightweight trail shoes; Skopelos' donkey paths and Skyros' rocky trails aren't kind to flimsy soles.

And ladies, pack a sarong—it doubles as a beach cover-up, picnic blanket, or makeshift curtain if your ferry cabin's window is stuck open.

Gear: Adventure-Ready Essentials

Island-hopping here isn't just about beaches—it's a choose-your-own-adventure of snorkeling, hiking, and scootering. Bring a reusable water bottle (refill stations are everywhere) and a collapsible tote for impromptu market runs.

If you're diving in the Marine Park, pack aqua shoes to avoid urchin spikes, and a microfiber towel—it dries faster than your average beach towel and fits in your daypack.

For hikers, a compact first-aid kit and a portable charger are lifesavers; trails like Skiathos' hidden coves can sap your phone battery (and your water reserves).

Sun Protection: Because the Aegean Doesn't Play Fair

Be warned: the sun in the Sporades is stronger than it looks. Even when it's cloudy, the UV rays reflect off the water and can sneak up on you. Use a reef-safe sunscreen with SPF 50+ (many locals love brands like *Ladima* or basic options from Greek pharmacies), and don't forget to reapply after swimming—nobody wants to go home with sunburned skin.

A wide-brimmed hat and polarized sunglasses aren't optional; they're survival gear.

Tip: Pick up a handmade *komboloi* (worry bead) bracelet from a Skyros market—they're not just stylish, they double as a fidget toy during sunburn-induced meltdowns.

Tech & Extras: Stay Connected, Stay Safe

Wi-Fi in the Sporades is... let's say, "charmingly inconsistent." A portable power bank is your new BFF for navigation apps on hikes or translating menus.

If you're renting a scooter (hello, Skiathos!), a GoPro or phone mount turns your commute into an action movie.

And don't forget a money belt for stashing cash—ATMs on Alonissos are as rare as a quiet day on *Banana Beach.*

Local Hacks You Won't Find in Guidebooks

Scooter Savvy: Rent one with a helmet that actually fits—Skiathos' hairpin roads are no joke.

Beach Buddies: Pack a mesh laundry bag for sandy swimsuits; it's a game-changer.

Taverna Ready: Bring a lightweight shawl or collared shirt—some traditional spots still frown on tank tops.

When in Doubt, Channel Your Inner Local

Still stressing? Take a cue from the islanders: they layer, they adapt, and they always carry a *koulouri* (sesame bread) for snack emergencies.

Leave the "just in case" items at home—your Airbnb host will lend you a wine opener, and the corner store sells SPF.

The Sporades aren't about everything being flawless—they're about going with the flow and enjoying whatever comes your way.

So, bring only what you need, be thoughtful about what you pack, and make sure there's space in your bag for a jar of Skyros honey or a bottle of Alonissos olive oil.

Greek Basics & Etiquette (Key Phrases, Tipping, Dress Codes)

The Sporades aren't just picture-perfect spots for your social media—they're real places where people live, and they take pride in warmly welcoming visitors.

If you want to fit in (or at least not look like a total tourist), here's a quick guide to common local phrases, how tipping works, and why you might want to save that skimpy swimsuit for certain areas only.

Greek 101: Phrases That'll Make Locals Beam

You don't need to recite **Homer,** but tossing out a few Greek words works magic. Start with *"Yassas"* (hello/goodbye) and *"Efharisto"* (thank you)—locals will practically throw ouzo at you.

If you're on Skyros, sprinkle in *"Kalimera"* (good morning) to farmers at the market, or *"Endaxi"* (no problem) when your taverna order gets mixed up.

Tip: Greeks love it when you butcher their language with a smile. Just don't overdo it—nobody needs a tourist shouting *"Opa!"* unironically.

Tipping: The Art of the "Fakelaki"

In the Sporades, tipping isn't just about cash—it's a tiny ritual. Here's the drill:

Restaurants: Round up the bill or leave 5–10% if service isn't included.

On Skopelos, your waiter might hand you cash mid-meal for change—don't panic, it's normal.

Taxis: Round up to the nearest euro (e.g., 12.50€ becomes 13€). Drivers on Skiathos know every backroad shortcut, so reward their GPS-defying skills.

Hotels: A euro or two per day for housekeeping—leave it tucked under the *komboloi* (worry beads) on your pillow.

Boat Crews: If you're diving or sailing, tip guides 5–10€ per person. They'll remember you next time you're snorkeling with sea turtles.

Dress Codes: Bikinis, Breezes, and Byzantine Respect

The Sporades vibe is "island casual," but context is queen. On the beach, rock that neon bikini—Banana Beach on Skiathos is your runway.

Off the sand, throw on a linen shirt or sundress. Locals might side-eye bare shoulders in churches or monasteries (hello, Skopelos' **Agios Ioannis** chapel from **Mamma Mia**!).

Skyros' festivals? Cover those knees and shoulders—traditional villages like Molos still honor old-school modesty.

Tip: Pack layers. Meltemi winds can turn a sunny hike into a shivering ordeal faster than you can say *"Where's my jacket?"*.

Cultural Nuances: What Not to Do

Punctuality: Greeks run on "island time." If you're late for a dinner reservation, blame the ferry. But don't test this at the airport.

Bargaining: Haggle at markets (Skyros' pottery stalls expect it), but never over food or services. That octopus you're grilling cost someone hours of labor.

Gifts: If invited to a home, bring dessert (baklava) or a bottle of wine. On Alonissos, a bag of coffee beans is the ultimate "thank you".

Photos: Always ask before snapping pics of people, especially elders. And no, that fisherman mending nets doesn't want his photo traded for a euro.

Island-Specific Quirks

Skiathos: Nightlife is king, but don't stumble into a *kafeneio* (coffeehouse) before noon—old-timers take their frappés seriously.

Skopelos: Respect the quiet hours (2–5pm) in residential areas. Those cobblestone streets echo, and your Airbnb host will hear your TikTok dances.

Alonissos: The Marine Park has strict rules—no touching coral, feeding fish, or leaving trash. Locals are eco-warriors; follow their lead.

Skyros: During the **Anastenaria** fire-walking festival (May 21–23), dress conservatively and keep your "*oohs*" and "*aahs*" respectful—it's a sacred ritual.

Final Tips

Learn the coffee code: "*Nero*" (water), "*Ellinikos*" (strong Greek coffee), and "*Freddo*" (iced anything) are survival phrases.

Embrace the chaos: Ferries run late, tavernas run out of moussaka, and goats might block your scooter path. It's all part of the charm.

Smile: Greeks read energy like the back of their tzatziki-stained hands. A warm grin goes further than a perfect "*Efharisto*".

GETTING THERE & AROUND

International Access (Flights to Athens/Thessaloniki, Onward Connections)

Touching down in Greece is your first step toward the Sporades' sun-drenched shores. Most international travelers fly into Athens (ATH) or Thessaloniki (SKG), the two main hubs with seamless connections to the islands.

Athens is the larger airport, offering more global flights, while Thessaloniki is a solid alternative for those prioritizing northern Greece. From either city, you'll need to pivot to the islands—here's how locals do it:

Fly Direct to Skiathos (JSI): The only Sporades Island with its own airport, Skiathos, is a game-changer.

Several airlines run seasonal flights from Athens or Thessaloniki (under an hour), making it the fastest entry point.

Book early in summer—these flights fill up fast, especially in July and August when the islands buzz with life.

Ferry It Up: If you're craving a slower, scenic route, ferries are your friend. From Athens, head to Volos or Agios Konstantinos ports, both linked to the Sporades via regular services.

Volos, a 3.5-hour drive from Athens, offers daily ferries to Skiathos, Skopelos, and Alonissos. For Skyros, the easternmost island, catch a ferry from Kymi in Evia (a 2-hour drive from Athens) with *Skyros Shipping Co.*— their boats zip you to Skyros in under 2 hours, with stops at Skopelos and Alonissos along the way.

Thessaloniki travelers can bus or drive to Trikeri port for ferries to Alonissos and Skyros.

Domestic Flights + Ferry Combos: Don't discount flying into smaller airports. From Thessaloniki, charter flights or buses to Nea Anchialos (near Volos) connect you to ferries. If you're eyeing Skyros, the Kymi ferry is the most reliable year-round option, as flights to Skyros's tiny airport are limited.

Onward Connections: Mastering the Hop

Once you've landed in Greece, timing is key. Ferries from Volos to Skiathos take 2 hours, while Skopelos and Alonissos add another hour. Check schedules via *Ferryhopper* or *Greece Ferries* —summer routes are frequent, but winter services thin out.

For Skyros, the Kymi ferry is a lifeline, departing daily in peak season (June–September) and less so off-season.

Carry-On Wisdom: Pack light for ferry-hopping— luggage space can be tight. Locals advise arriving 30 minutes early for smooth boarding, and if you're hauling a bike or gear, reserve space in advance.

Getting Around the Islands: Wheels, Waves, and Wanderlust
Skiathos: Bus It or Scoot

Skiathos is the most tourist-friendly, with a bus network that's a breeze to navigate. The main route runs every 15 minutes from *Skiathos Town* (Bus Stop 1) to *Kalamaki Beach* (Bus Stop 25), costing just a few euros.

 Renting a car or scooter here is a breeze too, though parking at popular beaches like *Koukounaries* gets competitive by midday.

Skopelos: Twists, Turns, and Taxis

Skopelos's mountainous roads are stunning but tricky. Buses connect the port (Glossa) to Skopelos Town and beaches like *Stafylos*, but services are sparse outside summer.

Most visitors choose to rent a car or an ATV to handle the sharp, winding roads—locals recommend **Skopelos Car Rentals**, since they bring the vehicles straight to the ferry port.

Taxis are an option, but they can be expensive, so it's a good idea to agree on the price before you start your ride.

Alonissos: Slow and Serene

Alonissos is blissfully quiet, with buses linking Patitiri (the port) to villages like Old Chora and beaches such as *Leftos Gialos*. Buses run every 1–2 hours in summer, but renting a scooter or bike gives you freedom to explore hidden coves.

Driving here feels like a rural escape—roads are narrow, so take it slow.

Skyros: Horseback and Hybrid Rides

Skyros mixes rugged terrain with unique charm. Buses connect the port (Linaria) to Skyros Town and beaches, but renting a hybrid bike or scooter is the local way to roll. For a quirky twist, try a horseback ride through the countryside—Skyros ponies are iconic.

Island Hopping Like a Pro

Ferries are the heartbeat of Sporades travel. Routes between Skiathos, Skopelos, and Alonissos run daily in summer (2–3 hours between islands), while Skyros requires planning due to its distance.

Book tickets online to avoid queues, and aim for morning departures to dodge afternoon meltemi winds that sometimes delay crossings.

Chauffeur Services & Private Transfers

If you're splurging, private transfers (via *The Thinking Traveller* or local operators) handle luggage and logistics, ideal for groups or families. Some hotels even offer free port pickups—always ask when booking.

Final Tips

Download FerryScanner for real-time updates—ferry schedules shift with weather.

Avoid driving in Skiathos Town's narrow streets; park at the port and walk.

In Skopelos, ask rental agencies for automatic cars if stick shifts stress you out.

Charge your phone before road trips—some remote areas have spotty signal.

Ferries & Island Hopping (High-Speed Catamarans, Schedules)

The Sporades islands are a web of turquoise waters and pine-clad coasts, and hopping between them feels like unlocking a secret map—especially when you master the ferry routes.

People who live here know that hopping between the islands smoothly isn't just about good fortune—it's all about good timing, using the right apps or tools, and knowing which ferries are reliable.

Let's break down how ferry travel really works in this area, where fast catamarans and smart planning help travelers move between islands like a pro.

High-Speed Catamarans: The Need for Speed (and Savings)

If you're itching to bounce between Skiathos, Skopelos, and Alonissos without wasting daylight, high-speed catamarans are your best bet.

Operators like **Aegean Flying Dolphins** zip between these islands in as little as 15 minutes (Glossa to Skiathos), making it easy to squeeze in a morning swim on one island and a sunset dinner on another.

These sleek vessels are a game-changer, offering one-way fares from €20 —perfect for budget-conscious explorers.

Tip: Book online early to snag these rates, as seats vanish faster than ouzo on a hot day.

For longer hops, like Volos to Alonissos, conventional ferries take around 5 hours, but if you're short on time, splurge on a faster option. Just brace for a bumpier ride when the meltemi winds kick up—summer afternoons can get choppy.

Decoding Schedules: When to Catch Your Boat

Ferry schedules here are as predictable as a Greek grandmother's baklava recipe—mostly reliable but with occasional surprises. Routes between Skiathos, Skopelos, and Alonissos run daily in summer, with 2–3 sailings a day.

 The quickest route? Skiathos to Skopelos Town clocks in at 1 hour, while Alonissos to Skiathos takes 2 hours.

 Skyros, the outlier, requires more planning: Ferries from Kymi (on Evia) to Skyros take under 2 hours but run only a few times weekly outside peak season.

Locals really recommend using *FerryScanner* or *Ferryhopper* for live ferry updates—make sure to install these apps before you leave home. Why? Because ferry times can change depending on the weather, and during summer, even last-minute cancellations can sometimes happen.

Try to book morning ferries to avoid delays caused by wind and to steer clear of the busy afternoon rush.

Booking Like a Boss: Skip the Queue

Gone are the days of queuing at ticket booths. Most ferry tickets can be booked online through platforms like *Ferries.co.uk* or direct via operators' websites.

For the Volos to Skiathos route (2 hours) or Agios Konstantinos to Skopelos (3 hours), booking 24–48 hours ahead is smart.

If you're hauling gear—like a bike or SUP—reserve space early; high-speed boats have limited storage.

Some of the smaller ferries only take cash, so it's a good idea to have some on hand. But if you're booking tickets online, credit cards are usually accepted.

If you're traveling with a group, you can also opt for private transfers through services like *The Thinking Traveller*, which takes care of all the details—though it'll be more expensive.

Island-Specific Hacks

Skiathos: The hub of the Sporades, Skiathos has the most frequent connections. Use it as your base to day-trip to Skopelos or Alonissos.

Skopelos: Ferries dock at Glossa or Skopelos Town. From Glossa, the 15-minute dash to Skiathos is ideal for a quick escape.

Alonissos: The slowest island to reach (5 hours from Volos), but its laid-back vibe makes the trip worth it.

Pair your visit with a stop at the *Marine Park* — accessible only by boat.

Skyros: The forgotten island. Ferries from Kymi are your lifeline, but flights are scarce. Time your arrival to catch the **Skyros Shipping Co**. boat, which stops at Skopelos and Alonissos en route.

When Things Go Off-Script

Even the most carefully made travel plans can run into problems. If a ferry gets canceled because of bad weather, try not to stress. Locals usually find a way around it—like renting a car and heading to a different port, for example from Volos to Agios Konstantinos, or catching a bus to Thessaloniki to explore other options.

Flexibility is your superpower here.

Final Wisdom from the Ferry Gods

Pack snacks—ferry food is overpriced and underwhelming.

Arrive 30 minutes early to snag a good seat (upper decks have the best views).

Charge your phone before boarding—some boats have USB ports, but don't count on them.

Traveling between the Sporades islands isn't just about moving from one place to another—it's about enjoying the whole experience. With fast catamarans speeding across the Aegean and ferries that feel like sunset cruises, each trip becomes a memorable part of your adventure.

Local Transport (Buses, Taxis, Rental Cars/Scooters, Bike Options)

The Sporades islands may be tiny, but their ways of getting around are just as special as the places themselves. Whether you're zipping through Skiathos' pine-covered woods on a scooter or holding on tight during a Skopelos bus ride with all its sharp turns, traveling here is all part of the fun.

Locals have figured out how to mix practicality with personality—here's how you can do it too.

Skiathos

Skiathos is the most tourist-friendly island, and its bus system is a well-oiled machine. The main route snakes from Skiathos Town (Bus Stop 1) to *Kalamaki Beach* (Bus Stop 25), with buses departing every 15 minutes in summer.

A single ride costs just a few euros, and you'll share the ride with sunburned travelers and chatty locals.

Tip: Avoid the midday rush to *Koukounaries Beach*—parking there gets as crowded as a Mykonos nightclub. For ultimate freedom, rent a car or scooter (€20–€30/day).

Just don't attempt driving in Skiathos Town's narrow streets; park at the port and explore on foot instead.

Skopelos

Skopelos' rugged terrain makes buses a slower affair. The main line connects Glossa (the port) to Skopelos Town and beaches like *Stafylos*, but services dwindle outside summer.

Locals skip the wait and rent cars or ATVs (€35–€50/day) to tackle the island's twisty roads—**Skopelos Car Rentals** even delivers to the port.

If you're brave enough to drive, brace for hair-raising cliffs and goats blocking the road. Taxis exist but charge premium rates; negotiate fares upfront or book via your hotel.

Alonissos

Alonissos is the Sporades' laid-back soul, and its buses reflect that. Routes link Patitiri (the port) to Old Chora and beaches like Leftos Gialos, but buses trundle along every 1–2 hours.

To unlock hidden coves, rent a scooter (€15–€20/day) or bike—narrow roads mean cars are more hassle than they're worth.

Tip: Fuel up early; gas stations are scarce, and running out of petrol on a remote road is a rite of passage you'll want to avoid.

Skyros

Skyros marches to its own drum. Buses connect *Linaria* (the port) to Skyros Town and beaches, but the real local move is renting a hybrid bike (€10/day) to explore the island's lunar-like landscapes.

For a taste of tradition, saddle up on a Skyros pony — these sturdy horses have been island icons for centuries.

Taxis are available but pricey; book ahead through your accommodation to avoid scrambling.

The Scooter Chronicles: Your Ticket to Freedom

Across all islands, scooters are the undisputed kings of convenience. In Skiathos, they're the easiest way to hit **Lalaria Beach** (only accessible by boat or scooter).

On Skopelos, they're a must for reaching **Panagia Monastery** without a 40-minute bus wait.

Just remember: helmets are mandatory, and renters will ask for your passport. Locals also advise booking early in summer—popular spots like *Koukounaries* see scooter shortages by midday.

Taxis: Worth Every Euro (Sometimes)

Taxis aren't cheap, but they're lifesavers for late-night returns from tavernas or hauling luggage. In Skiathos, a ride from *Koukounaries* to town costs ~€10.

On Alonissos, taxis wait at the port, but agree on a fare before hopping in. For groups, private transfers via companies like *The Thinking Traveller* include port pickups and hydrofoil combos—a splurge, but stress-free.

Bike It Like a Local

Biking is bliss on flatter islands like Skiathos and Skyros. Rent hybrids or e-bikes to cruise the **Achladies Bay** promenade or explore Skyros' salt flats.

On hilly Skopelos, stick to electric bikes—trust us, those mountain roads are no joke.

Always check brakes and gears before renting; some older bikes are better suited for museum displays than roads.

When in Doubt, Walk (or Swim)

Some corners of the Sporades are best explored on foot. Old Chora on Alonissos is a maze of stone houses begging for a stroll, while Skopelos Town's cobblestone alleys are scooter-unfriendly.

And don't forget—on islands like Skiathos, boat taxis (€5–€10) offer quick hops to secluded beaches when buses feel too slow.

Final Tips

Download apps: FerryScanner tracks bus/ferry updates, and Google Maps works offline for driving.

Pack light: Buses and boats have limited storage—leave the oversized luggage at home.

Timing: Buses and ferries rarely run past midnight; plan your ouzo nights accordingly.

SKIATHOS

Highlights (Koukounaries Beach, Lalaria Cliffs, Nightlife)

Skiathos might be the smallest of the Sporades' main islands, but it packs a punch when it comes to unforgettable experiences.

People from around here like to say the island has two moods: peaceful and party mode. During the day, it's all calm with beautiful beaches lined with pine trees and quiet spots to relax. When the sun goes down, everything changes—bars and restaurants come alive, music fills the air, and everyone's enjoying drinks and good company. Let's explore what makes Skiathos such a standout destination in the Sporades.

Koukounaries Beach: The Crown Jewel

Start your journey at Koukounaries, Skiathos' most iconic beach—and for good reason. This stretch of golden sand meets turquoise waters so clear you'll want to fill a water bottle with them (though we recommend sticking to the free-flowing spring water from local taps).

The beach is part of a protected nature reserve, surrounded by fragrant pine forests that give it an almost tropical vibe. Locals advise arriving early to snag a prime spot, especially in July and August when the island buzzes with visitors.

For a unique twist, rent a kayak and paddle around the bay's hidden corners—just watch out for the occasional sea turtle gliding beneath your boat.

After sunset, the beach bars here crank up the music, blending chilled-out vibes with fire pits and cocktails that taste better with sand between your toes.

Scan code below for photos and videos of Koukounaries Beach

Lalaria Cliffs: Nature's Drama Unleashed

If Koukounaries is Skiathos' heart, the Lalaria Cliffs are its wild soul. Accessible only by boat (ferries from Skiathos Town run hourly), these towering white-rock formations rise like giants from the Aegean. The cliffs are part of a protected area, so while you can't climb them, you can gawk at their jagged beauty from the water or the small pebble beach below.

Locals whisper that the best time to visit is late afternoon when the sun paints the rocks in golden hues, making them glow like embers.

Be sure to check out the "*Blue Cave*," a secret little cave not far from here where the water glows an amazing blue color. It's the kind of place that looks almost too good to be true—so grab a waterproof phone case before you go so you can snap some pictures that'll leave your Instagram friends in awe.

Scan below for more on Lalaria Cliffs

Nightlife: Where the Island Comes Alive

When the sun dips, Skiathos Town shakes off its sleepy demeanor. The maze-like streets, lined with 19th-century whitewashed houses, become a playground for night owls. Start your evening at a *kafenio* (traditional café) sipping frappés or *rakomelo* (honey-spiced brandy) while nibbling on *dolmades* (stuffed grape leaves).

As the night progresses, head to the harborfront bars, where DJs spin everything from Greek remixes to international hits.

For a taste of authentic revelry, follow the crowds to "*The Street*," a pedestrianized lane packed with bars like **Jack's Place** and **Bourtzi**, where dancing on tables is encouraged.

Tip: Skip the overpriced clubs and ask locals about hidden garden parties—these pop-up events under the stars are where you'll find island regulars letting loose.

Beyond the Highlights: Local Secrets

While Koukounaries and Lalaria steal the spotlight, Skiathos has quieter charms too. Hike the trail from Troulos Beach to Mandraki (both top-rated spots) for a peaceful escape with views of the Aegean.

If you're into history, don't skip the **House of Papadiamantis** in Skiathos Town. It's a small museum honoring the island's favorite writer. You can see where he worked and discover what made him describe Skiathos as *"a place where the soul finds its rhythm."*

Beaches & Swim Spots (Megali Ammos, Banana Beach, etc.)

Skiathos' beaches are like its personality—diverse, vibrant, and impossible to forget. From windswept shores perfect for adrenaline junkies to hidden coves where the only noise is the whisper of pine trees, this island serves up a coastal cocktail for every mood. Let's spill the local secrets on where to dive in.

Megali Ammos: The Water Sports Playground

Just a 10-minute stroll from Skiathos Town, *Megali Ammos* is the island's answer to thrill-seekers. Its shallow, crystal-clear waters are a playground for stand-up paddleboarding (SUP), jet skiing, and even kitesurfing when the northern winds pick up.

Locals love this spot for its balance of convenience and action—grab a coffee from the beachfront café, then rent a kayak to explore the rocky outcrops nearby.

Tip: Visit in the morning before the breeze kicks in for calmer SUP conditions.

Scan code for more on Megali Ammos

Agia Eleni: Peace Under the Pines

If Megali Ammos is the life of the party, Agia Eleni is its laid-back cousin. Tucked on the west coast, this small bay is framed by pine forests that stretch right to the water's edge, casting dappled shade over the sand. The calm, turquoise waters are ideal for a leisurely swim or snorkeling—look out for tiny silver fish darting around the rocks.

Pack a picnic (and a good book) because you'll want to linger here all afternoon.

Scan below for more on Agia Eleni

Lalaria's Hidden Gems: Tsougria & Tripia Petra

Lalaria might be famous for its cliffs, but its lesser-known bays are where the magic happens.

Tsougria, a short boat ride from the main cliffs, is a snorkeler's paradise. The seabed here is dotted with colorful pebbles and marine life, and the lack of crowds makes it feel like your own private Aegean slice.

Nearby, **Tripia Petra** (Hole Stone) is a natural rock arch sculpted by the waves—swim through it at your own risk (the current can be sneaky!) for brag-worthy photos.

Locals suggest visiting in the late afternoon when the light filters through the arch, turning the water golden.

Mandraki Elias & Aselinos: Wind-Dependent Winners

Ask a local where to swim, and they'll probably ask, "What's the wind doing?" For south winds, head to *Mandraki Elias*, a sheltered bay with gentle waves perfect for long, uninterrupted swims.

When the north wind blows, *Aselinos* becomes the hotspot—its deeper waters stay calm, making it a favorite for serious swimmers. Both beaches are blissfully low-key, with just a taverna or two serving fresh myzithra cheese pies.

Tips for Beach-Hopping

Rent a scooter to reach hidden spots like *Kanapitsa* or *Achladies*, where the crowds thin out and the fish tavernas get friendlier.

Boat trips are the best way to discover inaccessible bays—opt for a private rental or join a group tour from Skiathos Town.

Water temps stay warm until late October, so don't stress if you're visiting in shoulder season.

Towns & Villages (Skiathos Town Waterfront, Papadiamantis Museum)

Skiathos Town isn't just a pit stop—it's the island's beating heart, where whitewashed buildings spill down a hillside to meet a harbor dotted with fishing boats and yachts.

This place hums with authenticity, blending old-world charm with the lively pulse of a community that still feels like a well-kept secret. Let's wander its streets and shores like a local.

Skiathos Town Waterfront

Start at the waterfront promenade, where the rhythm of island life unfolds. Fishermen mend nets beside bobbing boats, while the scent of grilled octopus from seaside tavernas mingles with salt air.

The locals really love the **Bourtzi Fortress**—an old Venetian castle from the 1200s that now hosts cultural events. It sits right at the edge of the harbor, so you can get a great view from the top. Pick up a frappé from a nearby stand, walk up the stone path, and take in the scenery.

Even when there's no concert going on, the sight of sailboats out on the water with pine-covered hills in the background is unforgettable.

For a taste of local flavor, follow the crowd to the hidden outdoor café at Bourtzi's tip.

This no-frills spot, with plastic chairs and checkered tablecloths, serves the island's best bougatsa (custard pie) and whispers of sunset cocktails.

Nearby, the **Agios Nikolaos Church** and **Clock Tower** isn't just a photo op—its bell tower offers 360-degree views, and the church's icons, painted in vivid blues and golds, are worth a peek.

Papadiamantis Museum

Hidden away in the winding streets of Skiathos' Old Medieval Town, the **Papadiamantis Museum** is a heartfelt tribute to the island's most celebrated writer.

Alexandros Papadiamantis, a 19th-century writer celebrated for capturing Skiathos' essence, lived and worked in this modest stone house. The museum feels frozen in time: his wooden desk faces the harbor, sunlight still spills through the same window that inspired his tales, and his handwritten manuscripts are displayed under glass.

Scan below for more on Papadiamantis Museum

Locals will tell you his stories are *"the island's diary"*—ask a guide to translate excerpts, and you'll understand why his phrases like *"the sea here sings lullabies"* still resonate.

Beyond the Waterfront: Hidden Corners & Local Lore

Skiathos Town isn't all postcard views—its backstreets hide stories. Wander past bougainvillea-draped homes to the Castle, a crumbling fortress where Ottoman and Venetian history collide. The climb is steep, but the reward is solitude and a perspective that hasn't changed in centuries.

Down below, the Old Port buzzes with fishermen selling their catch. Join them at dawn for a coffee at *Avlios Yard*—a courtyard café where locals debate politics over thick espresso.

When to Visit & Insider Tips

Mornings are magic here: Watch fishermen unload their nets at the port, then grab a *tiropita* (cheese pie) from **Bakaliko**, a grocery-turned-café beloved for its homemade snacks.

Evenings belong to the waterfront. Book a table at **Exantas Bar** – Restaurant on Megali Ammos beach for sunset dinners—order the *astakomacaronada* (lobster pasta) and thank us later.

Late-night? Follow the sound of laughter to Bourtzi's summer cinema, where films screen under the stars. Locals bring their own cushions—take the hint.

Culture & History (Venetian Ruins, Local Festivals)

Skiathos may be tiny, but it's packed with history and traditions that the locals take pride in. You'll see it in the old Venetian ruins and in the lively festivals where the whole town comes out to dance. This island doesn't just keep its past alive—it celebrates it every day. Let's explore what makes Skiathos so unique.

Venetian Echoes: Bourtzi Fortress & Beyond

The Venetians left their mark on Skiathos in the 13th century, and nowhere is this more evident than at **Bourtzi Fortress**.

Perched at the edge of Skiathos Town's harbor, this weathered stronghold once guarded the island from pirates and rival fleets. Today, it's an open-air stage where history and modernity collide.

Climb the stone steps at sunset, and you'll find couples snapping selfies against a backdrop of yachts and pine-covered hills—the same view Venetian soldiers once scanned for threats.

Locals joke that the fortress "*throws the best parties,*" thanks to its summer concert series featuring everything from traditional lyra music to jazz.

Don't miss the annual August full-moon party, where the ruins glow under moonlight and crowds sway to rembetiko tunes.

But Bourtzi isn't the only whisper of Venice. Wander the Old Medieval Town 's labyrinthine alleys, and you'll spot arched doorways and stone walls that hint at the island's strategic role in Aegean trade routes.

Ask a taverna owner about the **Castle** (Kastro), a hilltop ruin where Venetian and Ottoman influences overlap. The climb is steep, but the panoramic views and the eerie quiet—broken only by the wind—make it feel like stepping into a time capsule.

Festivals: Where the Past Dances with the Present

Skiathos' calendar is punctuated by festivals that blend ancient traditions with island-style revelry.

The standout is **Violin Days** in early September, when the town becomes a stage for folk musicians and dancers. Locals dressed in traditional *foustanela* (pleated skirts) and embroidered vests perform the *kalamatianos*, a circle dance that's as much about community as it is about music. Grab a glass of retsina and join in—even if you step on toes, the crowd will cheer you on.

Religious festivals are equally vibrant. On August 15, the **Dormition of the Virgin Mary** brings processions through Skiathos Town, with candles flickering and church bells echoing off the harbor. The real action, though, happens afterward: tavernas set up tables in the streets, grilling *souvlaki* and serving *tsipouro* (a fiery spirit) until dawn.

For a quirkier tradition, time your visit for Easter, when locals light bonfires on beaches to symbolize the resurrection—a spectacle that's equal parts sacred and surreal.

Living History: Stories in Stone and Song

Skiathos' history isn't just in museums—it's in the air. The island's strategic location made it a pawn in ancient power struggles, from its days in the **Athenian Delian League** (478 BC) to its brief autonomy after the *Peloponnesian War*.

You'll hear echoes of this past in taverna conversations, where elders debate whether Skiathos was "more Venetian or more Ottoman."

Tips for Culture Vultures

Time travel at twilight: The best photos of *Bourtzi Fortress* are at golden hour, when the stones turn honey-colored and the harbor lights twinkle.

Ask about hidden churches: Skiathos has over 300 chapels, many tucked into hillsides. Locals will point you to *Panagia Kechria*, a cliffside chapel with a Madonna icon said to grant safe voyages.

Eat with history: Dine at **Taverna Kounistra** , built into a 17th-century olive press. The owner loves sharing tales of the island's rebellions over plates of *taramasalata*.

Dining & Accommodation (Beachfront Tavernas, Luxury Resorts)

Skiathos isn't just beautiful to look at—it's the kind of place that makes you feel good all over, especially when it comes to food and where you stay. You can dig into charcoal-grilled octopus right on the beach or enjoy a glass of bubbly with an ocean view from a fancy room. No matter what you're in the mood for, this island knows how to treat you right. Let's take a look at the best spots to eat, drink, and rest like a local.

Beachfront Tavernas

The best meals on Skiathos are served with a side of salt air. **Bakaliko**, a fish taverna in Skiathos Town, is a local legend. Pull up a chair on their harborfront terrace and watch fishermen unload the day's catch—your dinner might still be swimming when you order. Their specialty? *Astakomacaronada* (lobster pasta), drenched in a rich tomato sauce that's been simmered for hours.

 Pair it with a crisp Assyrtiko wine and soak in the view of the *Bourtzi Fortress* across the water.

For a toes-in-the-sand experience, **Amfiliki Tavern** on *Megali Ammos Beach* is a must. Locals rave about their *souvlaki* and *taramasalata* (fish roe dip), but the real star is the setting: tables inches from the waves, with the scent of thyme from nearby hills mingling with the grill smoke.

Time your visit for sunset, when the sky turns pink and the owner brings out complimentary shots of *tsipouro* (a grape-based spirit) to toast the end of the day.

If you're willing to venture beyond the obvious, **Ergon** in Skiathos Town blends traditional flavors with modern flair. Think slow-cooked lamb with honey and rosemary or stuffed calamari drizzled with aged balsamic. The open kitchen lets you watch chefs work magic, and the rooftop seating offers a front-row seat to the town's nightly *volta* (stroll).

Luxury Resorts

Skiathos' luxury scene is all about understated glamour. **Skiathos Princess**, a beachfront resort on the southwest coast, feels like a hidden kingdom. Villas with private infinity pools blend into the pine-covered hills, and the spa uses olive oil and sea salt harvested from nearby Alonissos.

Scan code for more on Skiathos Princess

For a splurge, book a sunset dinner at their **Aegean Blue** restaurant—think seared scallops with saffron foam or lamb chops marinated in local herbs, all paired with sommelier-selected wines.

Closer to town, **Mandraki Club** combines chic suites with old-school Greek hospitality. The poolside bar shakes up basil-infused gin cocktails, and the breakfast spread includes honey straight from the owner's hives.

But the real perk? A private path leading to a secluded beach where towels are laid out and ice-cold Mythos beers await.

Local Eats Beyond the Beach

Don't overlook Skiathos' inland gems. **Kahlua**, a garden restaurant hidden in the Old Town, serves dishes like *giouvetsi* (oven-baked pasta with meat) under twinkling lights.

It's a favorite for romantic dinners, but arrive early— the courtyard fills up fast. For a quick bite, **Savor** offers creative takes on street food, like spinach pie with feta and pine nuts, best enjoyed on a bench overlooking the harbor.

Tips for Foodies & Travelers

Lunch like a local: Skip the tourist traps and follow the scent of charcoal to **Marmita**, a no-frills spot near the port where fishermen and shop owners gather for grilled sardines and tangy dolmades.

Dinner reservations: In summer, book waterfront tables at least a day ahead—spots like ***Exantas Bar – Restaurant*** on *Megali Ammos* fill up by noon.

Accommodation hacks: If luxury resorts are booked, consider guesthouses in Troulos. These family-run spots offer homemade breakfasts and easy access to quieter beaches.

Day-Trips & Activities (Boat Tours, Sea-Kayaking)

Skiathos might be your home base, but the real magic of the Sporades lies in its hidden corners—reachable only by boat or paddle. Locals will tell you the best way to experience the islands is to *"let the sea guide you."* Whether you're chasing the **Mamma Mia** vibes or gliding through secret coves, here's how to make the most of your island-hopping adventures.

Boat Tours: Beyond the Postcard Views

Boat trips from Skiathos are less about the destination and more about the journey. Hop on a *Mamma Mia*-themed cruise and you'll soon see why Skopelos' cliffs and Alonissos' turquoise bays inspired the movie.

These tours often include stops at ***Kelyfos Island***, a snorkeler's paradise shaped like a turtle, where the seabed teems with colorful fish. The locals really recommend the sunset cruises that stop near *Porto Karras*, a quiet bay with crystal-clear water so clean you can see starfish swimming below just from looking over the boat's edge.

Scan below for more on Kelyfos Island

If you're craving authenticity, join a small-group fishing boat tour. These skippers know every hidden cove, from **Glarokavos** (a rocky outcrop with emerald pools) to **Chrousso Beach** (a sliver of sand accessible only by sea).

Bring a snorkel—the crew will point out underwater caves and maybe even share a bottle of retsina as the sun dips.

Sea-Kayaking: Paddle into the Wild

For adventurers, sea-kayaking is the ultimate way to explore Skiathos' rugged coastline. Rent a kayak from *Megali Ammos Beach* and paddle south to *Troulos Bay*, where olive groves tumble down to the sea. The real thrill, though, is heading north to *Lalaria Cliffs*.

Yes, you can kayak to the base of those iconic white rocks—just mind the occasional swell. Locals recommend early mornings for calm waters and the chance to spot dolphins playing offshore.

If you're new to kayaking, join a guided tour. Operators like **Skiathos Sea Kayak** lead trips to Koukounaries' hidden coves and even offer moonlit paddles—gliding through bioluminescent waters is a surreal experience.

Tip: Pack a waterproof phone case and a sense of humor; getting splashed is part of the fun.

Tips for Unforgettable Days

Beat the crowds: Book boat tours early (10 AM departures fill fast) or opt for private charters. Locals love *Vromolimnos Beach* on Alonissos—a 30-minute sail from Skiathos—for its laid-back vibe and family-run tavernas.

Pack smart: Bring reef-safe sunscreen and a hat—some boats have limited shade.

Combine activities: Some tours mix kayaking with snorkeling or hiking. Ask about Skopelos' monasteries —a steep climb, but the views from *Moni Evangelistrias* are worth it.

The Unwritten Rules

Skiathians have a saying: *"The sea gives, the sea takes."* Respect their way of life by leaving no trace—pack out trash, avoid disturbing marine life, and always ask permission before beaching on private coves.

If you're lucky, a fisherman might invite you for an ouzo toast after a day on the water. Say yes.

SKOPELOS

Highlights ("Mamma Mia" Chapel at Kastani, Pine-Covered Hills)

Skopelos isn't just another Greek island—it's a postcard come to life, where pine forests tumble down hillsides to meet cobalt waters, and a certain movie chapel still hums with ABBA nostalgia.

Locals here balance pride in their island's fame with a quiet love for its unspoiled soul. Let's spill the secrets on how to experience Skopelos like someone who calls it home.

Kastani Beach & the "Mamma Mia" Chapel: Dancing Queen Vibes

You've seen it in *Mamma Mia!* —that cliffside chapel where *Donna* raced against time (and a broken goat cart). *Agios Ioannis Kastaniotis*, perched above *Kastani Beach*, is still the island's crown jewel.

The chapel itself is tiny, whitewashed, and blissfully simple, but the real magic is the view: a panorama of pine-covered hills melting into the Aegean.

Locals joke that the stairs to the chapel are "*the ultimate leg workout*," but the sunset photos from the top are worth every step.

Kastani Beach below is equally iconic. Its pebbly shore and turquoise waters were the backdrop for the film's "*Dancing Queen*" scene, and yes, you can still reenact

Meryl Streep's leap into the waves (though the water's a bit chilly before July).

Scan below for more on Agios Ioannis Kastaniotis

For a quieter moment, follow the path south to **Milia Beach**, a hidden gem framed by pine trees where the only crowds are the occasional loggerhead turtles.

Pine-Covered Hills: Hiking Through the Green Heart

Skopelos wears its nickname— *"the green island"*— proudly. Over 70% of its land is covered in pine forests, and the scent of resin hangs in the air like a signature perfume.

The best way to dive into this lushness? Hiking trails that crisscross the island. Locals rave about the path from Skopelos Town to Panormos, a 45-minute trek through olive groves and pine forests that ends at a beach so tranquil you'll half-expect a pirate ship to appear (*fun fact*: ancient pirates did hide here).

For a shorter stroll, try the route to the **Monastery of Evangelistria.** The climb is steep, but the 18th-century monastery—perched like an eagle's nest—rewards you with silence, sweeping views, and maybe a cup of mountain tea from the resident monks.

Keep an eye out for ancient stone bridges hidden along the trails; some date back to Byzantine times and are still used by shepherds.

Local Secrets Beyond the Spotlight

Skopelos has a special kind of charm that goes beyond its pretty views—it's all in the little things. You can rent a scooter (a lot of people recommend **Skopelos Moto**) and ride over to Loutraki, a quiet village where fishermen still fix their nets by hand and local tavernas dish out *spetzofai*—those hearty sausages with peppers—right from the pan.

If you're up for some exploring, track down the "*Pirate Graves*" near Glossa, a group of old tombs carved into the rock, showing that this island has been a secret hideout for ages.

Tips for Mamma Mia Fans (and Everyone Else)

Timing: Visit the chapel early (before 10 AM) to avoid tour groups and snag that perfect Instagram shot.

Pack a picnic: Stock up on local cheese and olives in Skopelos Town and eat under the pines at *Panormos Beach* —the tavernas there will even loan you a blanket.

Go off-road: Ask locals about *Antrines*, a secluded cove accessible only by foot or boat. The rocks here glow golden at sunset.

Beaches & Swim Spots (Milia, Panormos, Stafylos)

Skopelos' beaches are the stuff of daydreams—pebbled shores lapped by liquid sapphire, pine forests that tumble to the water's edge, and coves so quiet you can hear the breeze whispering through the trees.

People from around here like to say the island's beaches are a lot like its famous cheese pies—best enjoyed when you take your time. Let's check out three standout spots that show off Skopelos' charm, from glamorous views to hidden pieces of history.

Milia Beach

Milia is the island's crown jewel, and not just because it starred in **Mamma Mia.** This pebble beach is a masterclass in contrasts: the stark white stones against turquoise waters create a palette so vivid it feels painted.

Locals love it for its crystal-clear snorkeling —dive in and you'll spot schools of silver sargos fish darting around underwater rocks. The beach is blissfully uncrowded (even in peak season), but arrive early to claim a shady spot under the tamarisk trees.

For a post-swim treat, follow the path to **Milia Taverna**, a family-run spot where the octopus is grilled over charcoal and the tsipouro flows freely.

Ask the owner about the hidden trail to nearby **Perivoliou Beach** —a sliver of sand accessible only by foot, perfect for a sunset skinny-dip.

Scan for more on Milia Beach

Panormos Beach

Panormos is where Skopelos shows its romantic side. This horseshoe-shaped bay, framed by pine-covered hills, is famous for sunsets that turn the sky into a watercolor of pinks and golds.

The pebbly shore slopes gently into calm waters, making it ideal for families—or anyone who wants to float lazily while watching fishing boats bob on the horizon.

Locals pack picnics with Skopelos' famous myzithra cheese and fresh figs, then stake out spots near the chapel of **Agios Nikolaos**, which glows like a beacon at dusk.

For a dose of adventure, rent a kayak from the beach's rental shack and paddle to **Glysteri Beach**, a nearby cove with emerald waters and a solitary taverna serving *bougatsa* (custard pie).

Scan below for more on Panormos Beach

Stafylos Beach

Stafylos isn't just a beach—it's an open-air museum. Named after the ancient tomb of a legendary king (rumored to hold golden treasures), this sheltered bay blends myth with modern-day beauty.

The beach is made up of a mix of small rocks and rough sand, and the water is so clear you can see straight down to the bottom, even several meters deep. If you're into history, it's worth snorkeling around the rocky areas—there are rumors that ancient Mycenaean artifacts are still hidden underwater there.

After a swim, take a quick walk up to the *Stafylos* archaeological site, where old stone walls give you a glimpse into the island's long history.

For lunch, make your way to the village of Glossa, which sits on a hillside and has tavernas that serve up *spetzofai*—sausage with peppers—along with plenty of local news and chatter.

Scan below for more on Stafylos Beach

Local Secrets & Practical Tips

Getting around: Rent a scooter or ATV in Skopelos Town—the winding roads to these beaches are part of the adventure (watch for goats!).

Timing: Visit Milia in the morning for calm waters; save Panormos for late afternoon when the light is golden.

Eats: Skip the beach bars and follow locals to *Agnontas Taverna* near Panormos, where the *astakomacaronada* (lobster pasta) is legendary.

Towns & Villages (Skopelos Town, etc)

Imagine a whitewashed labyrinth where bougainvillea spills over stone walls, the smell of baking cheese pies wafts from bakeries, and the chatter of old-timers playing backgammon mixes with the clink of coffee cups.

This is the island's heartbeat, a blend of old-world charm and laid-back vibes. Let's wander its streets and stories like a local.

Skopelos Town: A Harborfront Haven

Start at the harbor, where fishing boats bob beside yachts, and the morning sun glints off the Aegean. Locals gather here at dawn to buy fresh *gavros* (anchovies) straight from the nets—a ritual that's been unchanged for centuries.

The town's maze-like alleys are a treasure hunt: peek into workshops where artisans shape ceramics using techniques from their grandfathers, or stumble upon hidden courtyards where women string beads for traditional *komboloi* (worry beads).

For a taste of local life, grab a seat at Taverna Agnanti, a family-run spot perched on the hillside. Their terrace offers panoramic views of the harbor, and the *spetzofai* (sausage with peppers) is legendary. Pair it with a glass of retsina and watch the sunset paint the sky in hues of apricot and lavender—a daily show locals never tire of.

Beyond the Town: Hidden Villages & Secret Views

Skopelos' charm isn't confined to its main town. Rent a scooter (locals recommend **Skopelos Moto**) and zip to Glossa, a hillside village dubbed *"the balcony of the Aegean"* for its jaw-dropping views. The streets here are lined with geranium-filled pots, and the **Church of Agios Ioannis** (a short hike above the village) offers a panorama that'll make you forget your Instagram filter.

For a quieter escape, follow the winding road to **Klima**, a fishing hamlet where colorful *syzitria* (traditional houses with sunken patios) cling to the cliffside. There are just a few tavernas around here, and they all serve octopus that's dried in the sun right on the rocks—a technique the locals say is the best way to keep that fresh ocean taste locked in.

Tips for Town-Hopping

Festivals: If you're here on August 15, join the **Dormition of the Virgin Mary** celebration—a mix of solemn processions and street parties with live lyra music.

Hidden gems: Ask about *Agnontas*, a tiny port south of town where fishermen grill octopus over coals and sell it straight off the boat.

Culture & History (Myth of Peparithos, Byzantine Churches)

Skopelos isn't just a pretty face—it's an island where myths breathe life into stones, and Byzantine churches stand like silent storytellers. Locals here don't just recite history; they live it, whether they're sharing tales of ancient kings or lighting candles in chapels older than most countries.

Let's uncover the legends and sacred spaces that make Skopelos a place where the past feels deliciously present.

The Myth of Peparithos: A King, A Tomb, and A Legacy

Skopelos' origin story revolves around **King Peparithos** (or **Staphylus**), a mythical ruler said to have given the island its ancient name, *Peparithos*. Even though experts aren't sure if he actually existed, the people who live here believe in the story: he was a Mycenaean hero, and they say his grand tomb is near Stafylos Beach.

The tomb, a short hike from the shore, is a humble pile of rocks today, but archaeologists found Bronze Age artifacts here—proof that Skopelos thrived over 3,000 years ago.

Ask a taverna owner about *Peparithos*, and they'll likely spin a tale of pirate gold hidden in the tomb or whisper that the king's spirit still guards the island's shores. Whether fact or fiction, the myth fuels Skopelos' identity. You'll see his name on menus (try *spetzofai "Peparithos-style"* with extra peppers) and hear his legacy in the lyra melodies played at festivals.

Byzantine Churches: Where Faith Meets Folklore

Skopelos' Byzantine churches are masterpieces of simplicity and survival. Tucked into hillsides or hidden in olive groves, these stone structures have weathered centuries of pirates, wars, and earthquakes.

Start at the **Monastery of Evangelistria**, perched like a fortress above Skopelos Town. Built in the 18th century, it channels Byzantine vibes with its arched doorways and frescoes of stern-eyed saints. The monks here still follow ancient rhythms—join them for sunrise prayers, and you'll feel the weight of tradition in every chant.

For a hidden gem, hike to **Agios Ioannis Kastaniotis**, the "**Mamma Mia**" chapel near *Kastani Beach*. While it's famous for ABBA dance-offs, few realize its Byzantine roots. The current chapel sits on ruins of a 12th-century church, and locals say the site has been sacred since pagan times—look for carvings of ancient symbols beneath the whitewash.

Living History: Festivals and Folklore

Skopelos' culture isn't locked in museums—it spills into the streets. On August 15, the island erupts for the **Dormition of the Virgin Mary**.

The faithful process through Skopelos Town carrying icons, while tavernas set up grills in the streets. It's a mix of solemnity and celebration, with *tsipouro* flowing freely and grandmothers teaching toddlers traditional dances.

Even quieter moments have history. Pop into **Panagia Faneromeni**, a tiny chapel near Glossa, and you might find a local woman lighting candles for her family. The church's faded frescoes depict scenes from Byzantine lore, and the view from its courtyard—over the Aegean to Alonissos—is a reminder of why the Byzantines called this region "*the divine coast*".

Tips for Culture Vultures

Ask about hidden churches: Locals take pride in their secret spots. **The Church of Agios Nikolaos** near Panormos Beach has a marble iconostasis carved by a 17th-century monk.

Combine myth and beach: After visiting Peparithos' tomb, swim at Stafylos Beach—the Mycenaeans believed its waters had healing powers.

Taste history: Try myzithra cheese at **Agnontas Taverna** —its recipe hasn't changed since Byzantine shepherds grazed goats on these hills.

Dining & Accommodation (Local Cheese Specialties, Seaside Hotels)

Skopelos doesn't just serve food and shelter—it serves experiences. This island is a place where cheese is an art form, tavernas feel like family reunions, and hotels blend into the landscape like seashells on a beach. Let's jump into the flavors and stays that make Skopelos unforgettable.

Local Cheese: A Love Affair with Milk and Tradition

Skopelos' cheese is the stuff of legend, and locals take their dairy seriously. The island's *myzithra* (a tangy, fresh cheese) and *mizithra* (a creamy variety) are staples, often served drizzled with honey or baked into pies.

You'll find the best versions at **Taverna To Souvlaki tou Sotiris**, where the cheese pie (tiropita) is so flaky, it's said to have been blessed by the gods—or at least by the owner, who's been perfecting the recipe for 40 years.

If you want to really experience the local flavors, stop by **Agnontas Taverna** near the small harbor it's named after. The myzithra cheese there is freshly made every day by shepherds from the hills and served with sun-dried tomatoes and olives—a mix that truly captures the taste of the Aegean.

While you're on the island, don't skip the cheese markets in Skopelos Town. Vendors there wrap slabs of graviera, a rich and nutty aged cheese, in fig leaves, a practice that goes all the way back to Byzantine times.

Seaside Dining

Eating by the water in Skopelos isn't just about the view—it's a full sensory experience. At **Margarita Restaurant** in Glossa, tables are set on a terrace clinging to the cliffside, offering views of Alonissos and the Sporades' *"divine coast"*.

Order the *spetzofai* (sausage with peppers) and a glass of local white wine, and you'll understand why this spot is a favorite for sunset dinners.

For a toes-in-the-sand vibe, **Taverna Agnanti** in Skopelos Town is magic. Their charcoal grill turns out octopus so tender, it practically melts, and the *taramasalata* (fish roe dip) is creamy perfection. But the real star? The sunset ritual —locals and visitors alike gather here to toast the day's end with ice-cold Mythos beers and plates of fried kefalotyri cheese.

Seaside Hotels

Skopelos' hotels aren't just places to crash—they're extensions of the island's soul. **Villa Calm** by **Petrino Villas** in Skopelos Town redefines luxury with private pools that blend into the hillside, offering uninterrupted views of the harbor. The minimalist design lets the Aegean light flood in, and the breakfast basket (delivered daily) includes honey from the owner's hives.

For a quieter escape, **Petrino Villas** in Klima offers whitewashed cottages steps from the water. Fall asleep to the sound of waves lapping against the cliffs, then wake up to a breakfast of *bougatsa* (custard pie) and fresh figs on your private terrace.

Scan below for more on Petrino Villas

Prefer something rustic? **Skopelos Moto** isn't just a scooter rental—they've partnered with family-run guesthouses in Glossa where you'll share breakfast with goats and grandmothers who still make yogurt the old-fashioned way.

Tips for Cheese Lovers & Hotel Hoppers

Cheese crawl: Start at **Panagiotopoulos Dairy** in Skopelos Town for a tasting, then follow the scent of grilled halloumi to **Rakomelo**, a hidden gem where cheese is served with honey and cinnamon.

Book early: Seaside hotels like **Villa Calm** fill up fast in July and August—locals recommend booking by April.

Ask for "off-menu" cheese: At Taverna **To Souvlaki tou Sotiris**, whisper the secret phrase "*Eho fagito gia* *ena filo*" ("I have a friend who eats") to unlock dishes like *kaltsounia* (cheese-stuffed pastries).

Day-Trips & Activities (Islet Cruises, Hiking Trails)

Skopelos is the perfect starting point for exploring the hidden gems of the Aegean. Whether you're heading out to quiet, untouched islands or hiking old paths once walked by shepherds and holy figures, every day trip here feels like uncovering a secret part of the Sporades. Let's take a look at how the locals make the most of their time on this island.

Islet Cruises: Sailing into the Blue Unknown

The Sporades' charm lies in its scattered islets, and Skopelos is the perfect base to explore them. Hop on a *Mamma Mia*-themed cruise and you'll glide past **Arkos,** a speck of land with pebble beaches and waters so clear you'll spot octopuses darting between rocks.

These tours often include stops at **Kelyfos Island** (Turtle Island), a snorkeler's paradise shaped like its namesake, where the seabed teems with neon fish.

The locals say the best way to explore is by renting a private boat—guys like *Spiros* from **Skopelos Tours** know all the secret spots, from the green-blue waters of Glysteri to the steep cliffs of Dassia, where wild goats keep an eye on you from the rocks above.

For a taste of the wild side, ask about **Marine Park** excursions to Alonissos. This protected area is a sanctuary for monk seals and dolphins, and cruising its waters feels like stepping into a nature documentary.

Pack a picnic (locals recommend myzithra cheese and figs) and anchor at *Peristera*, a deserted islet with a shipwreck visible from the surface—a hauntingly beautiful snorkel spot.

Scan below for Skopelos Tours

Hiking Trails

Skopelos' trails are where myths and nature collide. The path to the **Monastery of Evangelistria** is a pilgrimage in every sense. The steep climb through pine forests rewards you with silence, save for the breeze and the occasional bell of a grazing goat.

The 18th-century monastery, perched like a bird's nest, offers lemonade made by the monks and views that stretch to Alonissos.

 Locals time this hike for sunrise—when the sky turns gold and the Aegean seems endless.

For a gentler stroll, try the Skopelos Town to Panormos route. This 45-minute walk winds through olive groves and ends at a beach where pirates once hid loot.

Take a dip to cool off, then walk the path to *Milia Beach* for a scene straight out of **Mamma Mia**—no goat cart needed. If you're up for a serious hike, try the loop from Glossa to Klima, a trail along the cliffs with jaw-dropping views known as the *"Balcony of the Aegean."*

Tips for Unforgettable Days

Boat hacks: Book cruises early—spots on ***Mamma Mia*** Experience tours vanish fast. Bring reef-safe sunscreen; some islets have fragile ecosystems.

Trail wisdom: Wear sturdy shoes (paths can be rocky) and ask locals about hidden trails to Agios Ioannis — the chapel's stairs are steep, but the sunset views are legendary.

Combine activities: Pair a hike to Stafylos Beach with a swim—the Mycenaeans believed its waters held healing powers.

ALONISSOS

Alonissos is a peaceful standout—a place where you'll find beautiful natural scenery, clear blue waters, and a relaxed atmosphere. While nearby Skiathos is lively and crowded, Alonissos offers something more genuine and calmer, making it an ideal spot for those looking to unwind and truly experience the charm of the Aegean. Here's a closer look at why this island is so special and often overlooked.

Highlights (National Marine Park, Biosphere Reserve)

Imagine floating in water so clear it's like swimming in air, with steep cliffs dropping straight into the ocean around you. This is the experience waiting for you at **Alonissos' National Marine Park**—the very first protected marine area in Greece.

Spanning a whopping 2,260 square kilometers, it's not just a park—it's a lifeline for endangered species and a blueprint for marine conservation.

The star resident? The Mediterranean monk seal (*Monachus monachus*), one of the rarest mammals on Earth. Though spotting one is a stroke of luck (they're elusive and fiercely protected), knowing your visit supports their survival adds depth to every swim.

The Park isn't just about seals. Its seagrass meadows and coral reefs teem with life, making it a snorkeler's dream.

The people who live there really recommend taking boat tours that leave from Patitiri Harbor — skippers don't just steer the boat; they share tales about how the park came to be in 1992 and how limiting fishing helped protect the sea from being overused.

Ask nicely, and they might point out hidden coves where the seabed drops suddenly, revealing a kaleidoscope of marine life.

On land, Alonissos' wild soul shines. Hike up to Old Alonissos Town (Kastro), a cliffside maze of stone houses abandoned after an earthquake but still humming with history.

The Byzantines built a fortress here in the 13th century, and the views—from the pine-clad hills to the glittering Aegean—explain why. Locals often picnic here at sunset, unpacking spanakopita and laughing as the sky turns pink.

Wear sturdy shoes; the path is rocky, but every step is worth it.

The island's UNESCO Biosphere Reserve status means even the air feels different—clean, pine-scented, and alive. Keep an eye out for rare birds like Audouin's gull or the Eleonora's falcon soaring above the cliffs.

If you're lucky, a shepherd might wave you over to share a sip of *tsipouro* (a fiery grape spirit) and chat about life in this ecological sanctuary.

Beaches & Swim Spots (Agios Dimitrios, Marpunta Coves)

The beaches of Alonissos are more than just spots to take a dip—they're the kind of places you remember long after you leave. Say goodbye to crowded shorelines; here, you'll discover quiet coves so untouched they feel like your personal escape in the Aegean. Let's take a closer look at two favorite spots that both locals and visitors love.

Agios Dimitrios

If you're craving a beach that embodies the wild beauty of the Sporades, Agios Dimitrios is your answer. Tucked between rugged cliffs, this golden-pebbled shore is a stunner, with waters so clear they rival the Caribbean.

 The beach's unique "tongue" shape creates a sheltered lagoon effect, making it perfect for lazy floats or snorkeling among tiny silver fish.

 Don't let the pebbles deter you—locals swear they're easier on the feet than other rocky beaches, and the two beach bars mean you won't go thirsty.

Arrive early to snag a spot under one of the few umbrellas (yes, it's organized but blissfully low-key) or claim a patch of sun-warmed pebbles for an afternoon of people-watching Greek-style: think toddlers building sandcastles, fishermen mending nets, and elders sipping coffee in the shade.

Pack a picnic with local *tyropita* (cheese pie) from Patitiri and time your visit for sunset—the cliffs glow amber, and the sky puts on a show.

Marpunta Coves

For a mix of luxury and untamed nature, head to the Marpunta peninsula, where pine forests tumble down to meet the sea. This area isn't a single beach but a collection of hidden coves, each more enchanting than the last. The main Marpunta Beach is a pebbled gem with sunbeds and a chic beach bar serving icy ouzo cocktails.

But the real magic lies in exploring beyond—it's a 10-minute stroll along rocky paths to quieter inlets like *Chrisi Milia*, where golden sands meet emerald waters framed by olive groves.

Locals love this area for its dual personality: families flock to the calm, shallow waters near the **Marpunta Resort**, while adventurers' kayak to secluded bays or snorkel around the rocky outcrops.

The peninsula's pine-scented breezes and lack of crowds make it ideal for a midday siesta under the trees—just don't forget your sunscreen; the shade is sparse.

Alonissos' swim spots reward the curious. Rent a kayak from Patitiri to discover **Kalamakia,** a tiny cove with a seabed that drops suddenly into cobalt depths—perfect for cliff-jumping if you're brave.

Or ask a fisherman at **Leftos Gialos** (south of the island) about the best snorkeling spots; they'll point you toward reefs teeming with parrotfish and octopuses.

Remember: This island thrives on respect for nature. Avoid touching coral, use reef-safe sunscreen, and take your trash with you—locals take pride in keeping these beaches spotless.

Towns & Villages (Patitiri, Chora's Medieval Castle)

Alonissos might be small, but its villages pack a punch of character. From the lively hum of the port to the haunting beauty of a ruined castle, each settlement tells a story. Let's wander through Patitiri and Chora, where locals' lives unfold against a backdrop of history and salt-kissed simplicity.

Patitiri: The Island's Beating Heart (and Harbor)

If Alonissos were a song, Patitiri would be the upbeat chorus—the vibrant port village where ferries chug in, fishermen mend nets, and taverna owners wave you over like long-lost friends. As the island's administrative and commercial hub, Patitiri is where life feels most lived-in.

Its waterfront promenade buzzes with activity: cafes serve strong Greek coffee to old-timers debating politics, while kids splash in the shallows near the ferry dock.

Don't miss the **Archaeological Museum**, just behind the port. It's small but mighty, showcasing artifacts from ancient Ikos (Alonissos' ancient name), including pottery shards and tools that reveal the island's 5,000-year-old history.

Locals joke that the real treasure isn't inside the museum but outside—specifically, the fish market held every morning.

Arrive by 8 a.m. to see fishermen unload squid, sardines, and octopus straight from their blue-and-white kaiki boats. Even if you're not buying, the banter and briny aroma are quintessential Patitiri.

For a slice of local life, follow the smell of wood-fired ovens to *Megalochori*, a quiet neighborhood just uphill. Here, whitewashed houses with flower-filled balconies cluster around a tiny square. It's a world away from the port's bustle—perfect for sipping retsina under a bougainvillea-covered pergola.

Chora: A Ghost Village Steeped in Medieval Mystery

A 15-minute drive (or a scenic 45-minute hike) from Patitiri lies Chora, the island's soul-stirring medieval village. Abandoned after a devastating earthquake in 1965, this hilltop settlement feels frozen in time.

Crumbling stone houses cling to the cliffs, their terraces offering jaw-dropping views of the Aegean. At its heart looms the **Byzantine Castle**, built in the 13th century to fend off pirates. Though only fragments of walls and towers remain, the site exudes an eerie grandeur.

Locals call Chora a *"ghost village,"* but it's far from dead. Wander its labyrinthine paths, and you'll stumble upon restored homes now housing artisan shops and cozy *kafeneia* (coffee shops).

The Folklore Museum, housed in a 400-year-old mansion, offers a peek into traditional island life with exhibits on winemaking, weaving, and the island's seafaring past.

The best time to visit? Sunset, when the sky turns molten gold and the castle ruins cast long shadows over the village. Stay for dinner at one of the tavernas—To Kyma serves homemade *gemista* (stuffed vegetables) on a terrace overlooking the sea. Ask for a seat by the edge; the views are so vast you'll feel like you're dining on the edge of the world.

Village-Hopping Like a Local

Alonissos' villages reward the curious. In *Votsi*, a fishing hamlet near Patitiri, you can join fishermen at dawn to haul in nets or rent a boat to explore hidden coves. Meanwhile, *Steni Vala* on the east coast is a haven for sailors, with its protected bay dotted with yachts and seafood tavernas.

For a taste of island tradition, time your visit with **Panagia's Festival** in August, when Chora's square erupts with music, dancing, and copious amounts of *tsipouro* (a potent grape spirit).

Or swing by Patitiri's **Wine Festival** in September, where winemakers from across the Sporades pour samples of crisp *Assyrtiko* and velvety *Mavrotragano*.

Culture & History (Underwater Archaeology, Sea-Voyage Traditions)

Alonissos isn't just a pretty face—it's a storyteller. For millennia, its culture has been shaped by the Aegean's rhythms, from ancient sailors navigating by starlight to modern fishermen hauling in nets at dawn. Explore the island's deep connection to the sea, where every wave and rock tells a story rooted in history and tradition.

Underwater Archaeology: Sunken Secrets of the Aegean

Beneath Alonissos' turquoise surface lies a hidden museum—a treasure trove of shipwrecks and artifacts that reveal the island's ancient maritime prowess.

The National Marine Park isn't just a sanctuary for seals; it's a graveyard of historic wrecks, some dating back to the 5th century BCE.

 While snorkeling near *Peristera Islet*, you might glide over amphorae from a sunken merchant ship, their clay curves still intact after 2,500 years. Locals whisper that these waters hold stories of Byzantine traders and pirate raids, though many sites remain off-limits to protect fragile relics.

For a closer look, visit the **Museum of Alonissos** in Patitiri, a quirky gem founded by a local couple passionate about the island's seafaring past. Its piracy exhibit showcases rusted cannons, navigational tools, and even a replica of a 17th-century Ottoman galley—

proof that the island's history is as salty as its sea breeze.

Sea-Voyage Traditions: From Pirate Lore to Fishermen's Prayers

Alonissos has always been tied to the sea, and you can really see that in its culture. The island is home to Greece's only **Pirate Museum**, which tells the stories of corsairs who used to rule the Aegean long ago.

Housed in a restored stone building in Chora, it displays maps, weapons, and even love letters from infamous pirates who used Alonissos as a hideout. Locals joke that some families still trace their roots to these "gentleman thieves," who allegedly shared loot with villagers during hard times.

Today, traditions survive in quieter ways. Join fishermen at *Leftos Gialos* harbor before sunrise as they bless their boats with a spritz of holy water—a ritual said to ward off storms.

Or time your visit for August 15th, when the **Panagia Festival** erupts in Chora. Villagers dress in traditional white, dance the *kalamatianos* under the stars, and feast on *psaropita* (fish pie) to honor the sea's bounty.

Byzantine Echoes: Castles and Hidden Chapels

Alonissos' hills are dotted with reminders of its Byzantine golden age. *The Castle of Chora*, a jagged silhouette against the sky, was built in the 13th century to fend off pirates.

Wander its ruins at sunset, and you'll find fragments of frescoes in the tiny **Church of Agios Georgios** , where locals still light candles for safe voyages.

The island's spiritual heart beats in villages like *Steni Vala,* where the *Monastery of Evangelistria* clings to a cliffside. Its nuns brew herbal teas using recipes from Byzantine manuscripts and welcome travelers with stories of saints who calmed Aegean storms.

Living History: How the Sea Shapes Daily Life

You don't need a museum to feel Alonissos' history—it's alive in everyday moments. At Patitiri's fish market, grizzled captains sell octopus dried on ropes under the sun, a method unchanged for centuries.

In Votsi, women weave nets using techniques passed down from grandmothers, their hands moving like clockwork as they gossip in the shade.

Even the island's sustainable ethos has roots in tradition. The Marine Park's strict fishing rules mirror ancient practices where villagers rotated fishing spots to let stocks replenish—a wisdom modern scientists now applaud.

Dining & Accommodation (Eco-Lodges, Seaview Guesthouses)

Alonissos doesn't do dining or stays halfway. Here, meals are a celebration of the sea's bounty, and accommodations blend simplicity with soul-soothing views. Think tangled grapevines over your terrace, octopus drying in the sun, and guesthouses where the owner might just invite you for a nightcap. Let's unpack where to eat, sleep, and soak up the island's laid-back magic.

Dining: From Sea to Plate (No Filter Needed)

The food scene on Alonissos is like a heartfelt tribute to the Aegean Sea. A great place to begin is **Taverna Vasilis** in Patitiri, where *Maria*, a chef whose family has been cooking there for three generations, brings her grandfather's old recipes into the modern day.

Don't miss the *astakomakaronada*—think rich, creamy pasta with lobster that's so flavorful you'll be tempted to clean your plate with your fingers.

For a taste of tradition, head to **Kostas's Seafood Tavern** in Old Chora. *Kostas* himself hauls in the daily catch, grilling octopus so tender locals joke it *"melts before it hits the table"*.

Pair it with a carafe of house wine and a seat on the terrace overlooking the castle ruins.

Don't miss **Agiou Nikolaou Square**, the island's culinary heartbeat. Here, **Hayiati Patisserie & Piano Bar** serves *bougatsa* (custard pie) dusted with cinnamon, while **Kastro Restaurant** dishes up *tyropita* (cheese pie) flaky enough to rival the nearby Byzantine walls.

For a quick bite, pull up a stool at **Kóstas's Waterfront Café** in Patitiri (yes, another Kostas—this island loves its namesakes). His *kalamarakia* (fried calamari) and homemade lemonade have fueled fishermen and travelers alike for decades.

And if you're here in September, follow the smell of oregano to the *Wine Festival*, where winemakers pour velvety *Mavrotragano* and crispy *Assyrtiko* under the stars.

Accommodation: Where the Aegean Lulls You to Sleep

Alonissos' stays are less about luxury and more about living like a local. In Patitiri, Seaview Guesthouses line the harbor, offering balconies with front-row seats to the comings and goings of fishing boats.

These family-run spots are no-frills but full of heart—think hand-stitched quilts, geraniums on the windowsill, and fridges stocked with fig jam from the owner's orchard.

For a quieter vibe, Old Chora's stone cottages are a dream. Many were abandoned after the 1965 earthquake but have been lovingly restored with eco-friendly touches like solar-powered showers and reclaimed wood beams.

Wake up to the smell of wild thyme drifting through your window, then wander down to **Kastro Restaurant** for a breakfast of honey-drenched yogurt and sun-warmed figs.

On the Marpunta peninsula, eco-lodges blend into the pine forest, offering minimalist rooms with private decks overlooking hidden coves. Some even partner with the Marine Park for guided snorkeling trips—perfect for spotting seagrass meadows and (if you're lucky) a monk seal.

A few go the extra mile with sustainability: think rainwater harvesting, organic toiletries, and zero single-use plastic.

Hidden Gems & Local Secrets

The best meals often happen off-menu. At *Votsi Village*, ask fisherman-turned-taverna-owner *Giorgos* for the *psarosoupa* (fish soup)—a humble dish simmered for hours with saffron and tomatoes from his garden.

In Chora, **Hayiati Patisserie** doubles as a piano bar after dark; grab a brandy and request a song—the owner plays everything from rebetiko to Elvis.

For a splurge, book a room at Steni Vala's waterfront guesthouses. This sleepy fishing hamlet feels frozen in time, with rooms just steps from the bay.

Borrow a kayak from the owner and paddle to *Kalamakia Cove* at sunrise—it's a ritual that'll make you feel like the only person on the island.

Day-Trips & Activities (Marine-Park Diving, Blue Cave Tour)

The Sporades aren't just a cluster of islands—they're a playground for adventurers who crave the thrill of the deep blue and the sparkle of hidden caves.

Whether you're plunging into the Marine Park's protected waters or gliding into the legendary Blue Cave, these day trips are your ticket to the Aegean's wild side. Let's dive in, literally and metaphorically.

Marine-Park Diving

The Alonissos Marine Park isn't just a sanctuary for monk seals—it's a diver's wonderland. Strap on a tank and descend into a world where ancient shipwrecks mingle with vibrant seagrass meadows.

Local dive centers like those in Skiathos or Patitiri offer guided tours to spots like **Peristera Islet**, where a 5th-century BCE shipwreck lies encrusted with amphorae, frozen in time.

 The visibility here can hit 30 meters on a good day, making it feel like you're floating through an underwater museum.

But the real magic? Swimming alongside loggerhead turtles and schools of barracuda that dart like silver arrows. *"The Marine Park's rules keep these waters pristine,"* says a dive instructor who's been exploring these depths since the '90s. *"We're not just guides—we're guardians."*

Book a morning dive to avoid the meltemi winds, and finish with a seaside meze platter at Votsi Village, where fishermen will nod approvingly at your salt-crusted gear.

Blue Cave Tour

Picture this: your boat glides into a narrow inlet, and suddenly, the sea beneath you transforms into a neon blue mirror. Welcome to the *Blue Cave*, a natural wonder tucked into the cliffs of **Kira Panagia Island**.

Day tours from Skiathos or Alonissos often include this stop, pairing it with snorkeling at *Lalaria Beach* — a sliver of white pebbles framed by turquoise waves.

The best time to visit? Midday, when sunlight pierces the cave's mouth, turning the water into a glowstick of blues and greens.

The locals really recommend pairing your visit with a walk up to the *Byzantine Castle* in Chora if you're after a stunning sunset view. *"It's like the cave's colors follow you,"* laughs a tour operator who's been running boats since the '80s. *"You'll see them in your dreams."*

For a quirky twist, hop on a private yacht charter (prices start around €400 for a half-day) and ask the captain to detour to *Sarakiniko*, a pirate cove where the cliffs are so white, they look snow-dusted.

Beyond the Obvious: Hidden Gems for Curious Travelers

The Sporades' charm lies in its secrets. Ask around Patitiri's harbor for "hidden dives" —spots only locals know. One favorite is *Kalamakia Reef*, where the seabed drops sharply, revealing coral gardens teeming with parrotfish.

Or paddle a kayak to *Tsoukalia*, a secluded beach accessible only by water, where the sand is so soft it feels like powdered sugar.

For landlubbers, the Day Trip to Grenada (yes, the Caribbean-like islet, not the country) offers spice gardens and chocolate factories—a surreal contrast to the Aegean's salt-and-sage vibe.

 But the true local's pick? A sunset sail to *Tsangari*, a tiny island where goats outnumber people, and the only "bar" is a fisherman's cooler of Mythos beers.

Tips to Dive Like a Local

Book Smart: Day trips from Skiathos start at €25, but private tours (€35–€40) let you linger longer at hotspots.

Pack Light: Bring reef-safe sunscreen and a microfiber towel—locals hate single-use plastics, and so will you after seeing the Marine Park's beauty.

Timing: Avoid July–August crowds by visiting in June or September. The water's warm, and the light is golden.

SKYROS

Skyros is the Sporades' enigmatic outlier—a place where wild horses roam hillsides, villages cling to cliffs like something from a fantasy novel, and time slows to the rhythm of island life.

Larger and more remote than its neighbors, it's a mosaic of untamed landscapes and traditions that feel plucked from another era.

Let's uncover its soul through two icons: the mythical Skyrian horses and the labyrinthine charm of its villages.

Highlights (Skyrian Horses,etc)
Skyrian Horses: Tiny Titans of the Aegean

Imagine a horse so small it could trot under your kitchen table, yet so fierce it's been immortalized in ancient myths. The Skyrian horse, standing just 11 hands tall, is a living relic found nowhere else on Earth.

These pint-sized beauties have roamed the island's rocky slopes for over 2,000 years, believed to descend from steeds ridden by Achilles' warriors to Troy.

Today, they're protected in sanctuaries like the **Skyros Horse Trust**, where you can watch them gallop through olive groves or even join a guided hike to spot wild herds near Mount Kochylas.

Locals whisper that each foal is named after a Byzantine saint—a tradition as enduring as the horses themselves.

Scan for more on Skyros Horse Trust

Chora: A Village That Defies Gravity

Skyros' main town, Chora, is a masterpiece of cliffside engineering. Whitewashed houses with terracotta roofs cascade down a bluff crowned by a 13th-century Byzantine castle, creating a silhouette so dramatic it's been compared to *Game of Thrones* filming locations.

Stroll through the island's stone-paved streets, and you'll come across quiet little squares where older women still practice traditional weaving techniques passed down from their grandmothers.

Be sure to check out the **Archaeological Museum** too—it's housed in a Venetian-era house and displays old pottery and tools that tell the story of the island's long history at sea.

For the best views, hike up to the castle at sunset. As golden light spills over the Aegean, you'll see why pirates once coveted this vantage point—and why locals still gather here to gossip and sip *tsipouro* as the sky ignites.

Villages with Stories Etched in Stone

Outside of Chora, the villages on Skyros show how strong and enduring the islanders are. In Molos, along the west coast, you'll find a small group of stone houses where fishermen still fix their nets right by the clear blue sea.

It's also home to the **Monastery of Agios Nikolaos**, a 16th-century sanctuary where monks brew herbal teas using recipes from Byzantine manuscripts.

Meanwhile, **Kalamitsa** charms with its twin harbors and tavernas serving octopus dried in the sun—a delicacy paired with tangy kopanisti cheese.

Hidden Gems Only Locals Know

Skyros doesn't give up its secrets easily. Ask around for **Aspous Cove**, a sliver of pebbles and crystal-clear water framed by cliffs. It's blissfully quiet, save for the occasional fisherman hauling in nets.

For a quirky adventure, visit the **Skyros Pegasus Studios**, where artisans craft miniature replicas of the island's iconic horses—a perfect souvenir.

Foodies should time their visit for the **Panagia Festival** in August, when the island's patron saint is honored with feasts of lamb *kleftiko* (slow-roasted lamb) and dances that last until dawn.

And don't leave without trying strawberry spoon sweet, a tangy preserve made from the island's wild strawberries—a taste of Skyros in every bite.

Beaches & Swim Spots (Molos, Atsitsa, Achilli)

Skyros may be the Sporades' quieter, more independent island, but when it comes to beaches, it definitely doesn't hold back. Whether it's the busy sands of *Molos*, the secluded bays of *Atsitsa*, or the untouched charm of *Achilli*, Skyros offers a mix of coastal beauty that feels both rugged and inviting.

Let's explore the beaches that locals love and visitors can't stop talking about.

Molos: The Island's Pulse (and Party Central)

If Skyros were a song, Molos would be the upbeat chorus everyone knows by heart. This Blue Flag beach on the east coast is the island's social hub, where families, windsurfers, and sunset chasers converge.

 Its long stretch of golden sand merges seamlessly with neighboring *Magazia Beach*, creating a double dose of seaside bliss.

By day, rent a sunbed and watch kids build sandcastles while windsurfers carve up the waves—Molos' consistent breeze makes it a hotspot for watersports.

 By night, the beach bars come alive with bonfires and cocktails under the stars.

But Molos isn't just about crowds. Stroll north toward **Agios Nikolaos Chapel**, and you'll find quieter pockets where the only soundtrack is the crash of waves.

Locals recommend **Taverna Akrogiali** for grilled octopus and a front-row seat to the island's most electric sunsets.

Atsitsa: Seclusion Meets Drama

If you're looking for peace and quiet, Atsitsa is the hidden gem of Skyros. Found along the island's wild northern shore, this rocky cove is surrounded by pine-covered hills and clear waters that range from bright turquoise to rich blue.

Accessible only by a rocky path or boat, it's a favorite among hikers and snorkelers eager to escape the crowds. The lack of amenities (no umbrellas or snack bars) adds to its charm—pack a picnic and claim a spot on the smooth stones.

The real magic? The view of Skyros Town perched on the cliffs above. As dusk falls, the castle ruins glow amber, and the sea mirrors the sky in a spectacle that feels almost private.

Tip: Combine your visit with a stop at nearby *Pefkos Beach*, a sandy strip shaded by tamarisk trees, perfect for a post-swim nap.

Achilli (Agalipa): A Hidden Gem for the Bold

If you're up for a challenge, Achilli —also called Agalipa —rewards the adventurous with one of Skyros' most pristine beaches. Located on the island's remote southwest coast, this sliver of sand is a sanctuary of shallow, azure waters and rocky outcrops that beg to be explored. The journey here is an adventure: a bumpy drive followed by a scramble over sun-bleached boulders.

But locals will tell you it's worth it. *"Agalipa's beauty is raw,"* says a fisherman. *"It's what Skyros looked like before tourists."*

Once there, snorkel around the rocks to spot rainbow-colored fish or sprawl on the sand, where the only footprints are yours. Just don't expect amenities—this is a *"pack in, pack out"* kind of place.

Local Secrets & Bonus Spots

Skyros' beaches thrive on serendipity. Ask around for **Aspous**, a windswept cove on the west coast where the cliffs meet the sea in a clash of white stone and blue.

It's ideal for photographers chasing dramatic landscapes. For a family-friendly alternative, head to **Kalamitsa**, a sheltered bay with calm waters and a handful of tavernas serving strawberry spoon sweet — a tangy local specialty.

Don't miss **Magazia Beach** at sunrise. Though technically part of Molos, its quieter southern end offers a peaceful start to the day. Grab a *freddo cappuccino* from the kiosk and watch fishermen mend their nets.

Towns & Villages (Chora's Winding Alleys, Kastro Ruins)

Skyros' Chora is more than just a town—it's like stepping into a maze of white-washed houses stacked along a cliffside, almost as if they're lined up like pearls on a necklace. The air feels alive with stories of pirates, poets, and long-held island customs.

Sitting high above is the old Kastro fortress, its worn stones watching over everything. This village is the soul of Skyros, where every corner you turn seems to uncover something new and surprising. Let's take a closer look at what makes it so special.

Chora

Wandering Chora's winding alleys feels like stepping into a mosaic of eras. The village cascades down a hilltop, its cobblestone paths snaking past bougainvillea-draped homes with terracotta roofs—a style so distinct it's been dubbed *"Venetian-meets-Aegean"*.

Locals joke that GPS maps fail here; the labyrinth is designed to confuse invaders, not tourists. Get lost intentionally—you'll stumble upon hidden squares where old-timers play backgammon under plane trees, and artisans carve wooden doves, symbols of peace and the island's seafaring past.

The Archaeological Museum is a place you definitely shouldn't miss. Housed in a beautifully restored Venetian-era mansion, it showcases artifacts dating back over 5,000 years, from old pieces of pottery to Byzantine religious icons.

But the real highlight might be the museum building itself—its arched doorways and painted ceilings still carry echoes of the Venetian rulers who once lived here.

Scan for more on The Archaeological Museum

If you're there, ask the person in charge about the "hidden" rooftop terrace—you'll get a great view of the Kastro ruins in the distance.

Kastro: The Ruin That Watches Over Time

Sitting at the highest spot in Chora, the Byzantine Kastro stands like a broken stone crown of old walls and fallen towers. It was built back in the 13th century to protect the island from pirates, showing how strong and determined the people of Skyros have always been.

Though not much remains today—just some worn-out fortifications and a single little chapel—locals say the best part is the view. From up there, you can see the Aegean Sea stretching out forever, and the village beneath looks like a scattered pile of sugar cubes.

Time your visit for sunset when the sky ignites in golds and pinks, and the meltemi wind carries the scent of thyme from the hills.

Stay after dark (the site is open late in summer) to see Chora's lights twinkle like a constellation—a ritual that makes even jaded traveler's gasp.

Beyond the Castle Walls

Chora's soul lives in its details. Peek into courtyards where women weave Skyrian textiles, using patterns unchanged for centuries. These geometric designs, dyed with local herbs, adorn everything from tablecloths to the island's famous miniature horse blankets.

For a taste of local life, join the evening *volta* (stroll) along the *Plateia Dhorou*, where kids chase cats and tavernas serve *marathopita* (fennel pie) under strings of fairy lights.

Don't miss the **Church of Agios Nikolaos**, hidden near the Kastro. Its 16th-century frescoes, though faded, still glow with the intensity of a bygone faith.

Locals' light candles here before weddings or fishing trips—a tradition blending superstition and spirituality.

Villages That Orbit Chora's Charm

While Chora steals the spotlight, nearby villages add their own flair. *Magazia*, a stone's throw from Molos Beach, is a sleepy hamlet where fishing boats bob beside turquoise waters. It's also home to the **Monastery of Agios Nikolaos**, a 16th-century retreat where monks brew thyme-infused teas and share stories of pirate raids.

To experience something different, take a walk up to *Pouria*, a small group of stone houses surrounded by olive trees. Here, life moves at a slower pace, marked by the sound of goat bells and the clinking of coffee cups at the village's only café.

The people here talk about *"to kalo,"* which means *"the good life"*—a simple, peaceful way of living that really captures the spirit of Skyros.

Culture & History (Local Customs)

Skyros is more than just a beautiful island in the Sporades—it's like an open-air museum where old customs and everyday life go hand in hand. Whether it's locals shaping clay into handmade crafts or lively festivals that turn whole villages into celebration spots, Skyros' culture is rich with history, strength, and happiness.

Let's take a closer look at what makes this island so unique and full of character.

Festivals

Skyros' calendar revolves around festivals that blend pagan roots with Orthodox zeal. The crown jewel is the **Panagia Festival** in August, honoring the island's patron saint. Villages erupt with music, as locals clad in traditional *vissinos* (a red sash) and embroidered skirts dance the *kalamatianos* under strings of lanterns.

 The air smells of lamb *kleftiko* slow-roasted in wood-fired ovens and strawberry spoon sweet, a tangy preserve unique to Skyros.

But the real showstopper is **Apokreas** (Carnival season), when the island's men transform into *yeros* (old men) and *koreles* (young girls), wearing goat-hair capes and bells to chase away winter spirits. This ancient ritual, rooted in fertility rites, culminates in a bonfire where revelers jump flames to purify their souls.

Local Customs

Skyros' customs are a blend of practicality and mysticism. Fishermen still bless their boats with holy water at Leftos Gialos harbor, a ritual said to calm storms.

In villages like Pouria, women weave textiles using patterns unchanged for centuries, each geometric design a silent prayer for protection or prosperity.

Even the island's Skyrian horses play a role. Locals believe these tiny steeds carry the spirit of Achilles' warriors, and seeing one galloping freely is considered good luck.

Hidden Layers

Skyros carries its history in every part of its land. The old Kastro walls in Chora, built by the Byzantines to keep pirates away, still show marks left by attacks from both the Venetians and Ottomans. Walk along those ruins as the sun sets, and you can almost feel the past pressing down on you—locals like to say that every stone remembers every soldier and sailor who ever set foot here.

The Archaeological Museum in Chora adds context, displaying pottery shards and tools from 5,000 years of seafaring life.

The real history lesson, though, happens outside. Take a hike up to **Mount Kochylas**, where shepherds still herd their goats, and you'll come across old threshing floors and olive presses—proof of Skyros' long-standing connection to the land and its traditional way of life.

Dining & Accommodation (Family Tavernas, Boutique Hideaways)

Skyros doesn't just feed you—it nourishes your soul. Here, meals are a chorus of clinking glasses and shared stories, and stays are less about thread counts and more about waking up to the smell of wild thyme.

Whether you're breaking bread at a generations-old taverna or curling up in a boutique hideaway carved into the cliffs, this island turns travelers into honorary locals.

Family Tavernas

Skyros' tavernas are the island's heartbeat, where grandmothers rule the kitchen and every dish tells a story. Start at **Stefanos** in Chora, a family-run gem where the *agli-meatballs* (made from sea anemones) are legendary. "*My yiayia taught me to fry them until they're crispy but tender inside,*" says **Maria**, the third-generation chef, as she serves platters of these briny delights alongside tangy kopanisti cheese.

For a taste of tradition, hike to **O Mylos tou Balabani** in Kalamitsa, a windmill-turned-taverna where the owner grinds wheat into flour daily. Their lamb kleftiko (slow-roasted in parchment) falls off the bone, and the homemade strawberry spoon sweet is a revelation—tangy, sticky, and utterly addictive.

Don't miss **T'Adrachti** in Chora's maze-like alleys, a gyro spot where the souvlaki is charred to perfection and the tzatziki is flecked with wild herbs.

Locals know the best meals happen off-menu. At **Oi Istories tou Barba** (The Uncle's Stories), a rustic spot in Molos, the owner might pull out a bottle of *tsipouro* and share tales of his fishing days if you ask nicely.

Boutique Hideaways

Places to stay on Skyros are all about simple, heartfelt living. In Chora, small guesthouses like **To Skyriani** mix clean, modern design with the island's cozy charm—think bright white walls, handmade wooden beds, and balconies with views of the Kastro ruins.

Mornings begin with breakfast baskets of fig jam and sourdough delivered by the owner, a former sailor with a knack for storytelling.

If you're after some peace and quiet, make your way to *Kalamitsa Bay*, where old stone cottages are hidden in groves of olive trees. Places like **Stamatia** offer private pools and trails that lead directly to the shore.

The island's crown jewel? **Skyros Grand Hotel**, a 19th-century mansion transformed into a boutique retreat. Its terraces, draped in bougainvillea, offer panoramic views of the Aegean, while the poolside bar shakes cocktails infused with local herbs. It's the kind of place where you'll linger over sunset ouzo, wondering if the meltemi wind carries secrets from the nearby horse pastures.

Hidden Gems & Local Secrets

The best spots are often stumbled upon. In Pouria Village, **O Pappous Mou Ki Ego** (My Grandfather and Me) is a farm-to-table haven where ingredients come straight from the owner's garden. Try the *manites* (crab spaghetti)—a dish so fresh it tastes like the sea.

For a quirky stay, book **Villa Mantalena,** a cluster of traditional homes restored with eco-friendly touches. Solar-powered showers, organic toiletries, and zero single-use plastics make it a guilt-free escape. Plus, the owner's goats might just wander by your window at dawn.

Day-Trips & Activities (Horseback Tours, Mt. Kochila Hike)

Skyros isn't the kind of place you just visit—it's the kind of place you experience. And nothing gets you closer to the island's untamed heart than saddling up for a horseback tour or sweating your way up **Mount Kochila**. These adventures aren't just activities—they're gateways to understanding why Skyros feels like the Aegean's best-kept secret.

Horseback Tours: Gallop with Living Legends

The Skyrian horse may be small—only about 11 hands high—but it's much more than just a cute animal. It's a true symbol of Skyros itself. These fluffy-maned horses have been on the island for over 2,000 years and are thought to be descendants of the horses that once carried Achilles' soldiers into battle at Troy.

Nowadays, you can take rides through olive groves and along quiet paths with the **Skyros Horse Trust**, an organization dedicated to preserving this rare and cherished breed.

"It's not a pony ride—it's a partnership," says Anna, a local guide whose family has bred Skyrian horses for generations. Tours range from gentle walks for beginners to exhilarating canters for experienced riders, often ending with a picnic of local cheese and figs under a tamarisk tree.

For something a little different, try a horse-drawn cart ride through the stone streets of Chora—your horse might even stop to say hello to a taverna owner along the way.

The locals say the best time to go horseback riding is early in the morning, when the sun paints the hills in golden light and the only noises you'll hear are the rhythmic clatter of hooves and the faint jingle of goat bells in the distance.

Here's a tip: If you're visiting in late summer, sign up for a "herding experience," where you can join in the age-old tradition of helping move wild horses to new grazing areas—something Skyrians have done for generations.

Mount Kochila Hike

Skyros' highest peak, *Mount Kochila* (792 meters), isn't just a hike—it's a pilgrimage. The trail winds through ancient olive groves, past crumbling Byzantine chapels, and up a rocky spine that offers 360-degree views of the Aegean. *"You'll see why pirates feared this coast,"* says Yiannis, a shepherd you might meet along the way. *"The cliffs drop straight into the sea like a knife's edge."*

The hike starts near **Aghios Nikolaos Monastery**, a 16th-century sanctuary where monks still brew thyme tea using recipes from Byzantine manuscripts.

From there, the path steepens, passing shepherds' huts and terraced fields carved into the mountainside. Keep an eye out for hidden waterfalls in spring—locals say they're sacred, and some still toss coins into the pools for luck.

At the summit, you'll find the ruins of a Venetian watchtower and a windswept plateau where wildflowers cling to life.

On clear days, you can spot Skiathos and even the distant outline of **Mount Pelion** on the mainland. For the full experience, pack a picnic of kopanisti cheese and sourdough bread from Chora's bakery—your reward for burning 1,500 calories.

Local Secrets & Bonus Adventures

The best adventures in Skyros are the ones you stumble into. Ask around for hidden trails like the path to *Pefkos Beach*, where hikers cool off in turquoise waters after a sweaty ascent.

Or rent a bike to explore the island's interior, where villages like Pouria offer cold freddo cappuccinos and a chance to chat with farmers about their organic honey.

For a mix of culture and cardio, combine your hike with a visit to the **Faltaits Folklore Museum** in Chora. Housed in a 19th-century mansion, it showcases Skyrian life through the ages—including tools used to train horses and weave textiles.

The museum's owner, *Manos*, might even invite you for a shot of tsipouro if you ask about his grandfather's role in saving the island's horses.

SAMPLE ITINERARIES

7-Day Highlights Loop (Skiathos → Skopelos → Alonissos → Skyros)

Day 1: Skiathos

Begin in **Skiathos Town**, exploring its red-roofed harbor and the iconic **Bourtzi Fortress**.

Relax at **Koukounaries Beach**, renowned for its golden sands and pine-fringed shores.

Day 2: Skiathos → Skopelos (15 nm)

Sail to **Skopelos Town**, a postcard-perfect village with cobblestone streets and traditional architecture.

Visit the **Castle of Ghiža** for panoramic views.

Day 3: Skopelos

Hike the **Panagia Eleftherotria Monastery Trail** for lush landscapes and cultural immersion.

Swim at **Milia Beach** or **Agnondas Bay**.

Day 4: Skopelos → Alonissos (12 nm)

Arrive in **Alonissos**, part of Greece's first marine park. Discover the **Old Village** (Chora), abandoned after an earthquake and now partially restored.

Day 5: Alonissos

Snorkel in the crystal-clear waters of **Steni Vala** or explore the **National Marine Park** by boat, spotting rare monk seals.

Day 6: Alonissos → Skyros (35 nm)

Sail to **Skyros,** the southernmost Sporade.

Visit the **Palamari Archaeological Site** and the hilltop **Castle of Skyros**.

Day 7: Skyros

Explore the rural village of **Molos** or **Linaria**, then depart.

10-Day In-Depth Exploration
Day 1–3: Skiathos & Skopelos

Follow the 7-day loop but add a day in Skopelos for hiking the **Episkopi Gorge** and visiting the **Evangelistria Monastery**.

Day 4–6: Alonissos

Extend your stay to kayak around **Piperi Islet** (part of the marine park) and hike to the **Cave of Cyclops**. Participate in a cooking class using local ingredients.

Day 7–9: Skyros

Dedicate two days to cultural immersion: tour the **Archaeological Museum**, attend a traditional pottery workshop, and explore the **Kalamitsa Wetlands**.

Day 10: Return

Depart from **Skyros** or backtrack to **Skiathos** for flights.

14-Day Leisure & Off-Beaten-Path
Day 1–4: Skiathos & Pelion Peninsula

Spend extra days exploring Skiathos' hidden coves (e.g., Lalaria Beach via boat).

Sail to the mainland's **Pelion Peninsula** to hike **Mount Pelion** trails and visit Tsagarada's stone villages.

Day 5–7: Skopelos & Islet Hopping

Add a day trip to uninhabited islets like **Kyra Panagia** or **Psathoura**, ideal for secluded snorkeling.

Day 8–10: Alonissos & Rural Villages

Stay in **Kalamakia** or **Votsi** villages, interacting with locals and learning about sustainable practices in the marine park.

Day 11–13: Skyros & Cultural Deep Dive

Explore lesser-known villages like **Aspous** and **Agridia**.

Attend a **Skyrian Horse** farm visit, unique to the island.

Day 14: Departure

Return via ferry or flight from Skyros.

Notes: Itineraries are flexible; adjust based on ferry schedules (check locally) and seasonal availability (e.g., marine park tours in summer).

ACTIVITIES & EXPERIENCES

Beach-Hopping & Water Sports

The Sporades islands are a treasure trove of pristine beaches and thrilling water activities, blending adventure with relaxation.

Locals joke that the hardest decision here is choosing which beach to lounge on before noon—and they're not wrong. From Skiathos' iconic *Koukounaries Beach*, where golden sands meet pine forests, to Alonissos' secluded coves within Greece's first marine park, the islands cater to every vibe, whether you're chasing lively shores or serene escapes.

Skiathos: The Beach Hub

Start on Skiathos, the gateway to the Sporades, where **Koukounaries Beach** reigns supreme. People from around here really love the place for its clear blue water and beautiful green surroundings. But they'll tell you to get there early if you're visiting in July or August, otherwise it might be hard to find a good spot.

 For a quieter alternative, hop on a boat to **Lalaria Beach**, a hidden gem with pebbled shores and crystal-clear waves—accessible only by sea, it's a slice of paradise minus the crowds.

 Thrill-seekers can rent jet skis or join sailing tours from Skiathos Town, while sunset cruises offer a front-row seat to the Aegean's fiery skies.

Skopelos: Kayak & Cove Adventures

Heading north to Skopelos, the beaches get wilder. **Milia Beach**, with its emerald waters, is a favorite for snorkelers, while **Agnondas Bay** charms with its traditional fishing village vibe.

The best part of this place? Paddling out in a sea kayak. People who live here suggest going with a guide so you can check out secret sea caves and small islands like Kyra Panagia, where you'll usually be the only ones on the beach.

After paddling, refuel with fresh octopus at a seaside taverna—Skopelos' waterfronts are dotted with family-run spots serving catch-of-the-day specials.

Alonissos: Dive into the Marine Park

Alonissos is a haven for eco-conscious travelers. Its star attraction, the **National Marine Park**, protects rare monk seals and vibrant underwater ecosystems.

Snorkel or dive at **Steni Vala**, where the seabed teems with life, or join a glass-bottom boat tour to **Piperi Islet**, the park's crown jewel.

For a unique twist, hike to the **Cave of Cyclops**, a coastal trail offering jaw-dropping views, then cool off with a swim in the cave's hidden pool.

Locals also whisper about secret spots like **Leftos Gialos**, a beach accessible only by foot or boat, where the lack of cell service is part of the charm.

Skyros: Wild Beauty & Wetlands

Don't overlook Skyros, the southern outlier. Its **Kalamitsa Wetlands** are a birder's paradise, but the real draw is the rugged coastline. Beaches like **Molo**s mix fine sand with dramatic cliffs, while the uninhabited islets of *Skyropoula* and *Valaxa* nearby are perfect for day trips.

Windsurfing is popular here thanks to steady breezes, and traditional fishing boats (kaiki) offer sunset rides—ask captains about "secret" snorkeling spots they've frequented for decades.

Tips from Locals

Timing: Ferries between islands are frequent in summer, but double-check schedules in shoulder seasons.

Go green: The marine park in Alonissos enforces strict eco-rules—avoid touching coral, and always use reef-safe sunscreen.

Mix it up: Combine beach-hopping with water sports. On Skopelos, kayak to a remote cove, then picnic with supplies from a local bakery.

Hiking & Nature Walks

The Sporades are a hiker's dream, where trails wind through pine forests, olive groves, and coastal cliffs, offering solitude and staggering views. Locals will tell you the islands' rugged interiors are just as captivating as their beaches—and they're right.

Skiathos: From Peaks to Vineyards

Skiathos might be famous for its beaches, but its 200 km of hiking trails are a hidden gem.

The Aesthetic Forest, a protected area blanketed in Aleppo pines, is crisscrossed by routes like ST7 (Walking on the Peaks), which loops past the island's highest points and a family-run winery.

For a breezy coastal walk, tackle the **Koukounaries Trail**, which dips through dunes and ends at the iconic beach. Locals suggest downloading the *Skiathos Trails* app to navigate lesser-known paths like the **Monastery Route**, leading to the cliffside **Evangelistria Monastery**.

Tip: Springtime hikers might spot rare orchids along the way.

Skopelos: Gorges and Byzantine Secrets

Skopelos' 110 km of signposted trails blend history and nature. **The Episkopi Gorge**, a steep, rocky path near Glossa village, rewards adventurers with views of the Aegean and remnants of ancient stone bridges.

For a gentler stroll, try the **Skopelos Town to Velanio Beach** route—a 5 km amble past olive presses and Byzantine chapels.

Don't miss the **Panagia Eleftherotria Monastery Trail**, where hikers earn panoramic vistas and a cool drink from the monks' spring.

Locals warn that some trails are overgrown in summer, so ask at kiosks for updated conditions.

Alonissos: Wild Gorges and Monk Seal Territory

Alonissos' crown jewel is the **Kastanorema Gorge**, a rugged hike likened to Crete's *Samaria Gorge*. The trail follows a riverbed flanked by towering cliffs, ending at the marine park's edge.

For coastal views, hike from **Old Chora** (the island's abandoned, earthquake-ravaged village) to **Chrisi Milia Beach,** passing crumbling stone houses along the way.

The Piperi Islet Trail (part of the marine park) requires a guide but offers a chance to spot rare seabirds. Bring sturdy shoes—Alonissos' trails are rocky and unmarked in places.

Marine-Park Conservation Tours

The National Marine Park of Alonissos Northern Sporades isn't just a sanctuary for endangered monk seals—it's a blueprint for eco-tourism. Locals are fiercely proud of this protected area, and visiting responsibly is key.

Boat Safaris & Snorkeling

Join a glass-bottom boat tour from *Steni Vala* harbor to glide over Posidonia seagrass meadows, vital for marine life. Guides share stories of the park's 1,200-year-old shipwrecks and the critically endangered Mediterranean monk seal (locals call them monachus monachus). For snorkelers, Piperi Islet is a hotspot, but access is restricted—book tours that partner with the park's research team.

Kayaking the Protected Waters

Paddle through sea caves and hidden coves on a guided kayak tour. Routes often include *Kyra Panagia*, a uninhabited islet with a 12th-century monastery, and *Peristera*, where snorkelers can explore a 5th-century BC shipwreck.

Operators emphasize *"leave no trace"* ethics—expect to collect any trash you find along the way.

Citizen Science Opportunities

The Park runs seal-spotting programs where visitors log sightings via a mobile app. *"You're not just a tourist—you're helping protect these creatures,"* says a local biologist. Some tours include beach clean-ups or tree planting in erosion-prone areas.

Cultural Festivals & Local Events

The Sporades' calendar is packed with quirky festivals and traditions that let you dive into island life. Timing your visit around these events adds a layer of authenticity you won't find in guidebooks.

Skiathos: Night of the Dolphins

Every August, Skiathos Town hosts the **Agios Nikolaos Festival**, a mix of live music, seafood feasts, and a midnight swim at *Mandraki Beach* (rumored to be a dolphin hotspot).

Locals also celebrate **Eidomeni** in September, a harvest festival where tavernas serve free figs and honey-drenched *loukoumades* (doughnuts).

Skopelos: Chestnut Celebrations

In October, Glossa village erupts in the **Chestnut Festival**, with roasting pits smoking in the streets and competitions for the largest nut. It's a cozy, low-key affair—perfect for sampling *kastana* (chestnuts) and dancing to lyra music.

Alonissos: From Pottery to Poetry

The island's Old Chora **Cultural Nights** (July/August) feature open-air poetry readings in the ruins of earthquake-struck homes. For hands-on fun, join a traditional pottery workshop in Votsi village—locals still use techniques from Minoan times.

Skyros: Carnival Madness

Skyros' **Apokreas** carnival (February/March) is legendary. Locals dress as *yeros* (old men) and *koreles* (maidens), parading through Chora in colorful costumes. The festival peaks with the *Dance of the Sheep*, where villagers chase a woolly "king" through the streets.

Year-Round Hidden Gems

Cooking Classes: Skopelos' **Mama's Kitchen** workshops teach you to make *spetzofai* (sausage-pepper stew) using recipes passed down for generations.

Artisan Visits: On Skyros, tour the **Kalogerou Pottery Studio**, where 80-year-old Yiannis shapes amphoras using a kick-wheel.

Music Evenings: Alonissos' **Kalamakia Nights** feature fishermen singing *mantinades* (improvised rhyming couplets) over ouzo.

Insider Tips

Festival Dates: Many events are tied to Orthodox holidays, so confirm dates with local tourism offices.

Etiquette: At religious festivals, dress modestly (cover shoulders/knees) and accept offers of food—it's a gesture of pride, not politeness.

Transport: Rent a bike or scooter to reach rural events—some villages shut down roads during festivals.

The Sporades' blend of wild trails, conservation efforts, and vibrant traditions creates a travel experience that's both enriching and deeply personal.

PRACTICAL APPENDICES

Seasonal Weather & Sea Temperatures

The Sporades enjoy a classic Mediterranean climate—think sun-drenched summers, mild winters, and shoulder seasons that locals call "secret seasons."

From May to October, temperatures range from 25°C (77°F) in late spring to a sizzling 32°C (90°F) in July and August.

Sea temperatures hit their peak in August and September (24–26°C / 75–79°F), perfect for snorkeling or paddleboarding.

Summer (June–August) is the liveliest time, with bustling beaches and festivals, but savvy travelers know September and October offer warm seas and fewer crowds—ideal for hiking without the heat.

Winter (November–March) sees cooler temps (10–15°C / 50–59°F) and occasional rain, but Skopelos and Skiathos' pine forests turn lush and green, a stark contrast to their summer aridity.

Tips:

Pack layers for spring/fall hikes—mornings can be chilly even if afternoons warm up.

For diving or marine park tours, aim for June–September when visibility is clearest.

Ferry Timetables & Airline Contacts

Navigating the Sporades is part of the adventure. Skiathos is the transport hub, with frequent ferries to Skopelos, Alonissos, and Skyros. High-speed catamarans zip between islands in 1–3 hours, while traditional ferries (slower but scenic) are cheaper.

Summer schedules (June–September) are most frequent; in off-season, check locally as routes may shrink.

Key Routes:

Skiathos ↔ Skopelos: 15–20 minutes by speedboat, 1.5 hours by ferry.

Skopelos ↔ Alonissos: 30 minutes by ferry.

Alonissos ↔ Skyros: Limited direct ferries; often requires a transfer via Evia or Rafina (mainland).

Airlines: Skiathos' small airport (JSI) connects to Athens via Aegean Airlines and Sky Express —book early in summer.

Skyros has a seasonal airport (SKU) with flights from Athens, but ferries from Kimi (Evia) are more reliable.

Insider Hacks

Download *Ferryhopper* or *12Xpress* apps for real-time schedules and last-minute bookings.

For trips to uninhabited islets like Peristera or Kyra Panagia, join a sailing tour from Alonissos or Skiathos—they're only accessible by boat.

Sunday ferry chaos: Locals warn that weekend boats to popular islands like Skopelos fill up fast—arrive early or pre-book.

Greek-English Glossary

Navigating the Sporades is easier (and way more fun) with a few local phrases in your back pocket. Here's a cheat sheet to help you chat like a semi-local:

Basics

Hello/Yasou (Γειά σου): Use this for casual greetings—locals love it when visitors try!

Thank you/Efharisto (Ευχαριστώ): Essential after that extra spoonful of honey at breakfast.

Yes/Nai (Ναι) vs. ***No/Ochi*** (Όχι): Master these to avoid accidentally agreeing to a shot of ouzo at 9 a.m.

On the Trail

Hiking/Peripatos (Περίπατος): For asking about trails.

Mountain/Vouno (Βουνό): *"Is there a path up the vouno?"*

Map/Harti (Χάρτης): Keep this handy—some trails aren't marked.

At the Beach

Beach/Paralia (Παραλία): The go-to word for sandy shores.

Shoreline/Akti (Ακτή): Use this for rocky coasts or scenic walks.

Wave/Kima (Κύμα): Impress surfers by commenting on the kima size.

Water Sports

Sailing/Istiooploïa (Ιστιοπλοΐα): Book a trip using this term.

Snorkeling/Katadiptiri (Καταδυτήρι): Ask about gear rentals.

Kayak/Kano (Κανό): Paddle like a pro: *"Thelo na thimitho me kano!"* (I want to try kayaking!).

Food & Culture

Delicious/Nostimo (Νόστιμο): Praise your host's *spetzofai* (sausage-pepper stew).

Festival/Panigiri (Πανηγύρι): Ask, *"When's the next panigiri?"* to find local parties.

Tip: Greeks gesture a lot—nodding and saying *nai* ensures clarity. And if all else fails, smile and say *siga siga* ("slowly, slowly").

Emergency Numbers & Health Tips

The Sporades are safe, but it's smart to prep for surprises. Save these numbers:

Emergency Contacts

General Emergency/112: Works island-wide for police, fire, or ambulance.

Skiathos Police/24270 22222: For lost passports or scooter mishaps.

Skopelos Medical Center/24240 22222: Basic care; serious cases go to Volos (mainland).

Alonissos Health Clinic/24240 66666: Limited hours—confirm locally.

Health Hacks

Pharmacies/Farmakeio (Φαρμακείο): Look for the green cross. Many close for siesta (1–5 p.m.), so stock up on sunscreen (anthelios) and bug spray (antikounou) early.

Hydration: Tap water is drinkable, but bottled is safer (and cheaper from markets, not beach shops).

Sun Safety: Reapply SPF 50+—locals love *Sofradex* brand for burns.

Seasickness: Grab Stugeron tablets at pharmacies before boat tours.

Wildlife Watch: In the marine park, avoid touching coral or feeding seals—fines apply.

If you liked this book or it helped you plan your trip to the Sporades, I'd really appreciate it if you could leave a short review or share a quick rating! It would mean a lot.

Printed in Dunstable, United Kingdom